Lauren and Mallory enjoy a book together.

Marcus signs up for a literature circle.

Mallory and BJ discover orange while mixing paint for their pumpkins.

Our pumpkin patch.

Great Beginnings

Creating a Literacy-Rich Kindergarten

Resi J. Ditzel

Mililani Mauka Elementary School, Oahu, Hawaii

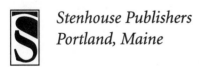

Stenhouse Publishers
Portland, Maine

Stenhouse Publishers, 477 Congress Street, Portland, Maine 04101

www.stenhouse.com

Library of Congress Cataloging-in-Publication Data

Ditzel, Resi J.
    Great beginnings : creating a literary-rich kindergarten program /
  Resi J. Ditzel.
      p.   cm.
    Includes bibliographical references.
    ISBN 1-57110-322-8
    1. Kindergarten—Curricula.   2. Curriculum planning.   3. Early childhood
education—Parent participation.   I. Title.

LB1180.D58   2000
372.19—dc21   00-036560

Cover and interior design by Catherine Hawkes, Cat & Mouse
Cover photograph by Resi J. Ditzel
Typeset by Technologies 'N Typography

Manufactured in the United States of America on acid-free paper
05 04 03 02   9 8 7 6 5 4 3 2

To Dad and Mom for our weekly trips to the library, which amongst other gifts instilled in me a lifelong love of learning.

To Myca and Jaryd for allowing me the great privilege of sharing with you a love and lifetime of learning similar to mine.

To Wayne for being my partner in life and learning.

CONTENTS

ACKNOWLEDGMENTS

GREAT BEGINNINGS IS A TEXT about how my students and I teach each other and learn together in my kindergarten classroom. The words in this story are mine; however, numerous perspectives, ideas, and voices were involved in this story. I am very appreciative of all the people who have contributed.

A very special thank you goes to Diane Stephens, who initially envisioned this book, for encouraging me to continue and expand upon this text. I will be forever grateful for her numerous contributions, tireless efforts, and dedicated work throughout my lifelong learning process. Diane will always be my mentor.

I would like to thank Wayne Suehiro and Donna Grace for all their input and insight. Their suggestions and comments were invaluable and used throughout this text. Thank you, Wayne, for all the late nights reading, questioning, and editing.

A big mahalo goes to all my new friends at Stenhouse, Philippa Stratton, Brenda Power, Martha Drury, and Tom Seavey. They have provided me with their immense talent, vision, energy, support, and patience. They have helped to me navigate through this new and difficult learning endeavor and opportunity.

I also would like to acknowledge my administrators, Betty Mow and Diane Ishii, my colleagues, Gail Ahina, Norene Lee, and Li-Anne Yoshimura, and my students for allowing me to use their work and ideas in this text. These people have been a continuous source of personal and professional support.

Finally and most important, I would like to thank the members of my family. Their constant support and understanding gave me the strength and courage to complete this text. I would like thank my husband, Wayne Suehiro; my son, Myca Ferrer; my parents, Fred and Jane Ditzel; my in-laws, Harry and Minako Suehiro; and Mary Matsuoka. Thank you for being my lifelong teachers.

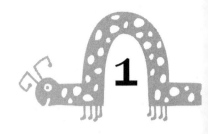

Welcome to Kindergarten!

BEING A KINDERGARTEN TEACHER is a tremendous responsibility. I am expected to provide twenty-five five-year-olds with a solid foundation and a great beginning to a lifetime of learning. For me, being a teacher is much more than just instructing students. It is about being a learner, asking questions, and growing together with the students. You will see throughout this book that the major emphasis in my classroom is on literacy, which is integrated with all content areas on each school day throughout the year. No matter whether I am teaching reading, writing, math, science, social studies, physical education, music, or art, I always try to integrate literature and ask myself the following questions:

What is my purpose?

What do I want the children to gain?

How can I make this meaningful?

How can I set this up so that the children will enjoy it?

How do I know that the children are learning?

In this book, which focuses on literacy, I detail my thoughts about planning and organizing my classroom and how classroom setup is related to my philosophy of how students learn. I continue by detailing my curriculum and my strategies to promote literacy throughout the daily schedule. Finally,

I share my belief that parents can be partners in the education of their children.

I hope that this book lets readers understand how I believe kindergarten children learn and that it serves as a practical and useful guide to teaching kindergarten.

I have been an elementary school teacher in Hawaii for twenty years. I have taught grades one, three, and five, and special education; however, most of my years as a teacher have been in a kindergarten classroom. I have learned a great deal through discussions with colleagues and authors. But I have probably learned the most from the children I work with—watching and trying to understand how they learn and then adjusting the curriculum to meet their needs.

Our school is located in the middle of the island of Oahu. It is a relatively new school, which opened in September 1993. We have over one thousand students from kindergarten through fifth grade, one class of special needs preschool students, and one fully self-contained class of children with special needs.

The families of our schoolchildren come from all economic backgrounds and a wide range of ethnicities. This diverse community provides many advantages, because students are exposed to various cultures and beliefs. And like other communities across the country, we face challenges, such as families with drug use, attention deficit with hyperactivity disorder, abuse, and emotional impairment.

Our students enter kindergarten with a range of experiences. Approximately five out of six children will have had some preschool experience: full-day programs, half-day programs, half-day programs meeting twice a week, and day care. Within a class, most of the entering students know their colors and can write their names, and possibly half know the alphabet and can count to ten. Some students are learning English for the first time. They experience the usual kindergarten anxieties, such as a new environment and leaving a parent for the first time, and in addition, nothing they hear makes any sense to them.

Within the classroom environment it is my job to find a way to make every child feel welcome and to make the curricular choices that will ensure everyone learns. Rather than start here by explaining why I teach the way I teach, I begin where most of my days begin—in the classroom with the children. By October, we've established our routines. We know and respect each other, and we work well as a community. This glimpse into my classroom also shows the realities of kindergarten teaching. Even though I have clear plans and expectations for each day, I also find there are many teachable moments that I need to grasp.

After describing a typical day, I explain how I lay the groundwork for the year in August and September (Chapter 2). The amount of planning and organizing that takes place in late summer is substantial, but it is essential for creating the environment in kindergarten where everyone feels valued and can learn new things.

I'M NOT SURE THERE IS any such thing as a typical day with a group of twenty-three five- and six-year-olds! But if there were, what might it look like?

My alarm goes off at 6:00 A.M. The weather report comes on: "High in the mid-80s, windward and mauka (mountain) showers, trades 10–15 miles an hour." The usual Hawaiian October day.

Having reassured myself that, as usual, we can expect a warm day without rain, I arrive at school at 7:00 and start opening up my room. I read through my mail and e-mail, feed the fish, take the chairs down from the tables, and straighten up a bit.

At 7:40, the children start to arrive. They know the rules. As is typical in most homes in Hawaii, the children remove their shoes and slippers before coming into the classroom. They line up outside and wait for me to open the door. As they wait, they wave at me through the glass window. I open the door at 7:45 A.M.

I stand at the entry and greet each child with a hug. This has always been my practice. I believe this is the best way to start the day because it puts each of my students at ease and helps them feel welcome and comfortable. As they come into the room, many of them are eager to talk to me. Amelia explains that her mother was rushing to work. She had been dropped off in the parking lot and for the first time walked to the classroom all by herself. I tell her that I am so proud of her. Spencer tells me that he wants to make a birthday card for his mother. I sing "Happy Birthday" and he laughs. Kara shows me a Pooh bandage covering a scrape on her foot. I take a look at her bandage and tell her it's a good thing she had such fancy bandages. The students are busily doing their "jobs," putting backpacks and books away and choosing a seat. At first, I had assigned seats to the students in order to build a sense of security and predictability. Now the students select their own seats.

7:55. The bell rings and school begins. Lauren jumps up and stands in front of the class. She is in charge this week and leads the students in the pledge of allegiance to the flag. After the pledge, looking around at the four table groups, she calls, "Table 3, please come to the floor . . . table 1, please come to the floor . . . ." Once they are all seated on the floor, Jaryd pops up to the front to lead the class in the Daily Calendar activities. He looks around at the students to make certain they are all listening to him. Walking over to the large calendar, he points to the date and says, "Today is October 9th. Yesterday was the 8th. Tomorrow is the 10th." He takes out the large class book and writes down what he has recited. The students assist Jaryd with the spelling. "T-O-D-A-Y space I-S space T-U-E-S-D-A-Y" they all chime together. One of the students reminds everyone that we are going to music class today. "You should write that down," Cori says. Jaryd records this event in the book. Jaryd walks over to the place value cups and adds a stick for the new day. Each stick represents one day of school. "How many days have we been in school?" he asks. Together the students count the sticks in the "tens" and "ones" cups. "Fifty-two" they count. Then Jaryd adds a tally to the chart, which keeps track of the number of days for that month. Math skills and concepts, including counting, numeral and number recognition, addition, and subtraction, are all incorporated into the calendar activities.

8:15. It's time for me to read aloud to the students. I usually select a literature book, a passage of poetry, or parts of a chapter book. I was planning to read a Halloween book but change my mind and read *Flower Garden* (Bunting 1994). In this book, a little girl and her father plant colorful flowers in a window box as a birthday gift for her mother. The students think the illustrations are beautiful. As I read, they wonder and whisper among themselves what will happen next. When I finish the story, Spencer immediately announces, "It's my mother's birthday today, too, like in the story." Just as I had planned.

8:30. Sharing or show-and-tell follows. Each student is assigned time to share once a week on a particular day. The students know which day of the week is designated for their turn. Today is Tuesday, and the first group can't wait to begin. Brad has brought an alligator's foot and a book about alligators that he got on his trip to Florida. Michellei shares a picture that she drew. Marcus has a container of little sea snails, seaweed, and sand that he picked up on the beach. Claire tells everyone that she had spaghetti for dinner. These "opening the day" routines provide a predictable structure for each morning.

8:50. Reading Workshop. Today I begin by sharing *The Farm Concert* (Cowley 1983). This book is perfect for my lesson. Yesterday, during Writing Workshop, several students had asked how to spell the word *said*. I decided that this would be a great time to introduce this word to all the students. *The Farm Concert* has the word *said* on almost every page. As we read the book together, we alter our voices to match the animal sounds. We laugh and laugh at how funny we all sound. Big Books are ideal to use because the students are able to see and read the large text

In the next part of Reading Workshop, the students read literature books from our classroom library. (A partial list of my classroom library books can be found in Chapter 3.) Sometimes they participate in Literature Circles and conduct Book Talks. I circulate among the students, talking to them about what they are reading, or I participate in a Literature Circle discussion. The students may also consult their reading folders, which contain songs,

Kelcie and Kim take turns reading aloud together.

rhymes, and poems that they have been learning throughout the year. Later today we will be adding a new song to their folders. Columbus Day is in a few days, and we will be doing some research and learning a song about Christopher Columbus.

9:10. The bell rings for recess. I hurry the students out the door. I want to send home my newsletter today and only have fifteen minutes to run to the workroom to photocopy it.

9:25. Back in the classroom, it's time for Writing Workshop. I like to start with a mini-lesson on a skill or concept that I want the students to understand or one that I have noticed through their writing they need to learn. Today I select the word *said.* I open *The Farm Concert* and say, "Let's see if we can find the word *said* on this page." The students immediately point to the word. "Good. How did you know that was the word?" I ask. I explain that sometimes words are spelled with letters that don't make that sound, so there are words they will just have to know by sight. After the mini-lesson, I encourage the students to apply the newly learned skill in their writing.

While the students are at their desks writing, I move among them and have conversations with them about their stories. Matthew is writing about the whales he saw off the coast in Maui. I ask him to tell me about his experience. He tells me about seeing the whales breach. As he is talking, he thinks of something he wants to include in his story. I move on. I'm not quite sure what Lise is writing and drawing. I say, "Tell me about your story." Lise tells me about how Princess Jasmine has met Cinderella. "That sounds interesting," I say. I accept all their ideas and encourage their best efforts. In this way, they become independent thinkers.

10:30. We're off to the dining room for early lunch. Our school has three lunch shifts, and we are in the first seating. A quick lunch with the other teachers, and it's time to pick up the students.

11:15. Back in the classroom again. Inquiry is next. I believe that it is a wonderful way to explore content areas such as science and social studies. Once we decide on the topic of study, I need to be aware of the students' prior knowledge and understanding. Today we decide to explore Christopher Columbus. I begin by asking what the students know about Columbus. Alex says, "Christopher Columbus sailed in a ship." Taylor says, "It was a long time ago." I ask what they are curious about and want to know about him. Kim wants to know if he is still alive. Chase is curious about where he lived. I record their responses on chart paper for all to use as a reference as we research this topic. This is a confidence builder for the students because they realize that I value their ideas and knowledge. I encourage them to participate and share with others. It also gives me a starting place for the research. If I did not begin with their prior knowledge, I might end up trying to reteach what they already know and understand. We read books and look through the computer encyclopedia for information on Columbus. We take a look at the map and locate the Atlantic Ocean and North America. Finally, I end by asking them what they have learned from the research on Christopher Columbus.

11:55. We bring out the reading folders, and I teach the song "Christopher Columbus." We learn to read the words in the song off a chart. I ask the students to tell me which of the words rhyme with *blue*. They draw a picture of something that reminds them of the song and add the song sheet to their reading folders.

12:10. Recess again. I double-check the schedule. Whew! No recess duty. While the students are outside playing, I gather my button box and book for the math lesson after recess.

12:25. That was a quick fifteen minutes. Time for math. Some of the math concepts are reinforced during the calendar activities at the beginning of the day. Others are introduced using literature. Today I read the book *The Button Box* (Reid 1990). In this book, Grandma's button box holds hundreds of different buttons. What a great book to begin a classification lesson. Shake, shake, shake. I shake the button box. BJ and Joleen's eyes widen. "What's in the box?" Micah wants to know. I open my button box and the students all let out an "ohhh." I begin this math lesson with the entire class. I grab a handful of buttons and place them on the floor. I begin sorting the buttons by color. I ask the students to tell me how I sorted the buttons. Kara says she can think of another way to sort the buttons and groups them by shape. Kelcie says she knows another way and sorts them by the number of holes in each button. "Terrific! How else can we group these buttons?" I ask. After working in a large group, I have the students work in small groups to explore and problem-solve. I always use manipulatives such as buttons to allow the students to learn by doing.

1:00. Time for the students to select a literature book for homework. "Yay, I knew we were going to get to pick a book now," Marcus calls out to me. "I'm going to choose your Birthday Book," I hear one tell another. They pack the books away in their folders and backpacks and get ready for the next activity.

1:05. "Can you read that Halloween book to us now?" Amelia says,

Taylor, Matthew, and Micah constructing a gear circus.

pointing to the book I had originally wanted to read. I respond that there is always time to read a book.

1:15. Elliott wants to know when we are going to have Centers. I guess we'd better make time for Centers now, before it's time to go home. I think it's row 2's turn today to select a center first. I carefully situate these centers according to function and availability of space. These centers promote socialization, intellectual stimulation, and problem solving. I have routines and procedures at the centers that are established from the first week of school. Today Dickson and Todd are having a disagreement in the Blocks Center. They both want to use the same truck. I know I don't need to intervene. The students are encouraged to reason and solve any problems themselves. They know they may ask me to help when they are unable to resolve the conflict themselves. I can hear them discussing the problem together. Dickson pulls out another truck, and it looks as though they have solved the problem. There are many problems that could arise during Centers because of the close interaction of the students in them. I always ask the students, "Tell me what happened when you tried to solve the problem." When students solve their own problems, a strong bond forms between the students, and classroom community is strengthened.

2:00. As the day ends, we gather on the floor. I encourage my students to assess what they learned and how they know they are learning. We talk about what was of interest to them and what they want to investigate further.

2:05. The bell rings. The students go to their cubbyholes and gather their belongings. I stand by the door as each student comes by and gives me a good-bye hug. They put on their shoes outside the door and turn for one more wave as they leave for the day. So ends a typical day. Boy, I'm tired!

MY STUDENTS GET TO THIS point of independence and feeling responsible for their own learning early in the year through a tremendous amount of modeling and patience. I keep a watchful eye on them and set the pace according to the needs and abilities of the group. I start off very slowly and structure a solid foundation with the students. It is vital to build a classroom community filled with trust, support, guidance, and security, which will create enthusiastic and self-assured learners. The students take ownership of their work and know I have complete trust in them. They have high expectations and confidence in themselves as learners. This book is the story of how we reach the point where most of our days can be "typical." This job begins early in the summer, when I begin to think about how to set up my classroom and plan for instruction on the first day of school.

Planning and Organizing

I ALWAYS STRIVE TO SET the right tone at the very beginning of the school year. I select the book *The Rainbow Fish* (Pfister 1992), which focuses on friendship and sharing, to begin the first day of school. This book is a wonderful choice for a first-day read-aloud. I get very large safety pins and slip on purple, blue, pink, and green beads, the same colors as the scales of the Rainbow Fish. I also put on one large, shiny, silver sequin, just like the shiny, silver scale of the Rainbow Fish. I come to school with these colorful, shiny scales pinned all over my clothes. The students' eyes grow wide as they are greeted in the morning by their sparkling teacher. We read and discuss the book, connecting its themes to our new classroom community. I give each student one shiny scale to help him or her remember to be a caring and sharing friend. It's a low-key, peaceful start to the school year—and that's all part of the plan.

I've learned that you need to take everything s-l-o-w-l-y at the beginning. Trying to cram all your ideas into one day is not going to make for a successful beginning. I take it slow and give the students a good, solid base on which to start the school year. When I take the time at the beginning, the rest of the year will be much easier.

My classroom is a predictable environment that encourages respect and security. This setting helps to develop independence, confidence, and risk taking, which is essential to active learning. By talking and listening to each other, we are all able to understand and accept different opinions and ideas. I set up this environment by my response to the students and through my actions. It is an ongoing process that continues to develop as the relationship between the students and myself grows.

I believe that routine schedules and structures are necessary in order for students to become risk takers and independent thinkers. I always build upon the prior knowledge of the students. I make certain they understand one concept before introducing another. The students gain respect for each other. I treat them as individuals filled with ideas and information that needs to be shared with the others. By giving them choice within the structure, I demonstrate my respect for them, and they become respected as individuals.

The planning for the school year takes place throughout the summer. I start by asking

How many students will I get this year?

What furniture arrangement will create the kind of classroom environment I would like for the students?

What will the traffic pattern be?

What kinds of centers do I want?

Which centers will work better next to each other?

Which objects will I label?

How will I make my students feel comfortable?

What kinds of homework do I want to send home?

As I'm thinking about the room arrangements and curriculum, I'm also thinking about my students. For some students, this will be their first day in a classroom. With no previous preschool experience, some will feel anxiety about the unknowns of schooling ahead.

Each year, I send home a letter to welcome the students to our new school. It is a wonderful way to introduce myself and make the students feel less apprehensive about coming to kindergarten.

Dear Myca,

Hi! My name is Mrs. Ditzel. I am going to be your kindergarten teacher this year. I am so happy that you will be in my class. We will have lots of fun at school together.

I am having a great summer. I went to see the Mulan movie. I loved it. Did you get to see it yet? I also went to see the Backyard Monsters at the Bishop Museum. That was really neat. I went to the tide pools at the beach, and I caught a crab, a sea cucumber, a brittle sea star, and some fish. What have you been doing over the summer?

I can't wait to meet you in August. See you then.

Love,

Mrs. Ditzel

This low-key, friendly start to the year is important for the tone I want to set in my classroom and the kinds of personal relationships I want to establish with my students. But I didn't know that at the outset. In my first year as a kindergarten teacher, I thought that I needed to cover lessons at a fast pace and the students would learn at the pace I set.

For example, one year on the first day of school, I had my students sitting on the floor in the front of the room. I proceeded to explain how they could make an apple out of construction paper. I told them how they could draw, cut, and glue the apple together. Then I sent them back to their desks to begin. Simple enough? What a mistake! I had students who had never held a pencil, never used a pair of scissors, and certainly never used glue before. I had paper being shredded, cut into bits and pieces, and torn with the misuse of those scissors. There was glue everywhere. I think one of the students actually used half a bottle on that one little piece of paper. What did I do wrong? I modeled for them. I demonstrated to them. Yet the lesson was a disaster. I stopped the lesson and read a book instead. That afternoon I did some reflecting and rethinking. The next day I decided to redo the lesson and take it step by step. I began by showing the students how to hold a pencil. I then had them go back to their desks and draw for me. Next, I showed them how to hold a pair of scissors, where to begin cutting, and how to follow along a curved line. Then I showed them how to open a bottle of glue so that just enough glue would come out, how much glue is needed, and where to place the glue. From that day, I realized how important it was not to rush through lessons just to get them done but rather to be assured that the students learn. I learned to watch the students and to teach to their needs and interests. I never make assumptions but teach and learn together with them.

Setting Up the Classroom

A good classroom arrangement will enhance learning and requires much thought and planning. I create a classroom arrangement that will work for the students as well as myself. The placement of the furniture is determined greatly by the location of the doors, windows, and chalkboard. I arrange my furniture so all of the students can work collaboratively and comfortably.

Table Arrangements

There are many things to consider when I arrange the furniture in my classroom. I find that clustering tables with four or six students works very well for collaborative group work. The clusters promote social learning and make the students feel more comfortable. They like knowing they have friends working and learning with them. I pay close attention to personality and compatibility. I assign seats at the beginning of the year. This gives students comfort and security in knowing exactly where they will sit each morning. However, a few months into the school year when the students have adjusted to our new classroom environment and school, I change their seating. At this point, they are free to choose their own seats. Each morning they may select a new seat. The only rule is that they may not sit next to the same person two days in a row.

Large-Group Area

I always set up a large-group area that accommodates the entire class. It is a gathering place for read-alouds, lessons, and Book Talks.

Center Arrangements

Each center is focused on a particular kind of activity and provides in one place the materials needed to carry out that activity. The activity may be carried out in the center itself or anywhere in the room. For instance, the Blocks Center is focused on building materials, and children are likely to use these materials in the Blocks Center itself. The labeling and chalkboard centers, on

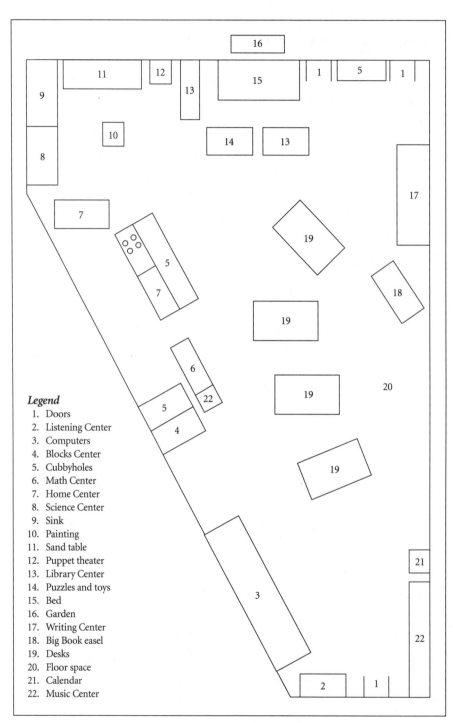

Layout in my odd-shaped classroom.

Legend
1. Doors
2. Listening Center
3. Computers
4. Blocks Center
5. Cubbyholes
6. Math Center
7. Home Center
8. Science Center
9. Sink
10. Painting
11. Sand table
12. Puppet theater
13. Library Center
14. Puzzles and toys
15. Bed
16. Garden
17. Writing Center
18. Big Book easel
19. Desks
20. Floor space
21. Calendar
22. Music Center

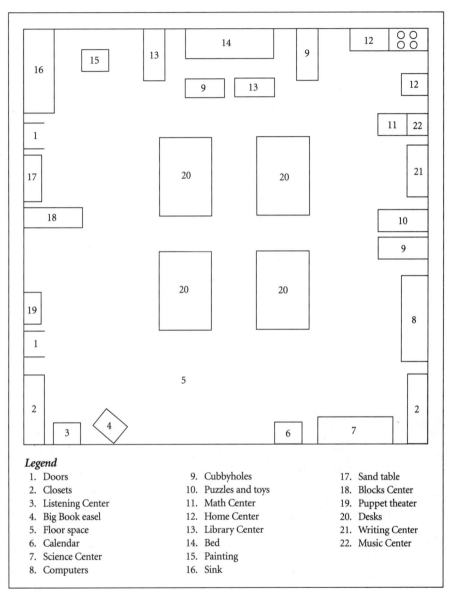

Layout in a rectangular classroom.

Legend

1. Doors
2. Closets
3. Listening Center
4. Big Book easel
5. Floor space
6. Calendar
7. Science Center
8. Computers
9. Cubbyholes
10. Puzzles and toys
11. Math Center
12. Home Center
13. Library Center
14. Bed
15. Painting
16. Sink
17. Sand table
18. Blocks Center
19. Puppet theater
20. Desks
21. Writing Center
22. Music Center

the other hand, provide materials for these activities in particular places, but the activities are carried out all over the room.

The centers are set up to focus on play and to promote social interaction. They provide the students with the opportunity to learn to cooperate and collaborate. The centers also aid the development of the students' academics.

I know my assigned room has an odd shape. I need to take this into consideration when deciding where to set up each center. Center arrangements will vary according to the space available and the physical layout of the classroom.

This year I decide to have the following centers:

* *Library Center* promotes reading and social interaction. This center includes fiction and nonfiction picture books, Caldecott award-winner books, predictable books, baskets of books sorted by authors, Birthday Books, magazines, newspapers, catalogs, a bed, pillows, and stuffed animals.

* *Writing Center* promotes reading and writing. I provide a table with a variety of paper, writing instruments, envelopes, a mailbox, stickers

Composing messages and letters in the Writing Center.

for postage stamps, a message board, and lists of students' and teachers' names with photos.

* *Listening Center* promotes reading and listening. A tape recorder, headsets, and taped stories are in this center.

* *Blocks Center* promotes social interaction, creativity, problem solving, reading, dramatic play, and experience with spatial relations. I include blocks, trucks, street signs, toy people, and enough floor space to create large structures.

* *Home Center* promotes social interaction, dramatic play, reading, and writing. I provide a stove, refrigerator, sink, hutch, table, chairs, pans, dishes, plastic food, clothing, stroller, shoes, telephone, paper, and pencils.

* *Music Center* promotes social interaction and concepts in music. I include rhythm instruments, music tapes, and an audiotape player.

* *Science Center* promotes problem solving, thinking skills, discovery, science concepts, reading, and writing. I provide a balance, live

Lauren takes a phone order in the Home Center restaurant.

Mallory and BJ discover patterns using shells in the Math Center.

creatures (crayfish, caterpillars, mealworms, fish), a magnifying glass, magnets (a horseshoe magnet, magnetic marbles, bar magnets, paperclips, coins, keys, metal washers), food coloring, jars of water, a center log, and pencils.

* *Math Center* promotes problem solving, thinking skills, understanding of math concepts, and social interaction. Pattern blocks, unifix cubes, geoboards, and boxes with junk (bread tags, small tiles, rocks, shells, keys, buttons, colored pasta, old clip earrings) are provided.

* *Computers* promote reading, writing, content area concepts, problem solving, and creativity.

* *Painting* promotes creativity, reading, writing, personal expression, and color mixing. In this center I have paper, paints, pencils, and a cookie sheet for mixing paint. The children have their own supplies like markers, crayons, and glue.

* *Sand/water table* promotes social interaction, dramatic play, problem solving, creativity, understanding concepts of conservation and reversibility (Piaget), and learning about physical properties of liquids and solids. I provide a sand table or container for sand, boats, graduated cups, measuring spoons, and variously shaped one-cup

containers. The sand/water table can hold either sand or water; part of the year I use water, part of the year I drain the water and add sand.

* *Puppet theater* promotes dramatic play, social interaction, comprehension of story, story sequence, and narrative structure. Included are a puppet theater, puppets, paper, and pencils.

* *Puzzles and toys* promote social interaction, creativity, problem solving, thinking skills, and experience with spatial relations. I include a table with puzzles, construction toys, gears, and unifix cubes.

* *Reading labels around the room* promotes reading. I include pointers and glasses without lenses like the ones worn by the children in the photograph on the cover of this book.

* *Writing/labeling around the room* promotes reading and writing. I provide paper to make labels, pens, tape, and clipboards.

* *Flannel board* promotes creativity, reading, and writing. A flannel board, felt letters, and felt pictures are available.

* *Chalkboards* promote reading and writing. I provide a container with individual chalkboards, chalk, and erasers.

Kara creates a modern art masterpiece with items from the Idea Box.

* *Magnetic board* promotes reading and writing. A magnetic board or file cabinet and magnetic letters are needed.

* *Idea Box* promotes creativity, problem solving, invention, and discovery. A large covered container with junk (paper, paper towel tubes, film containers, egg cartons, pieces of fabric, yarn, wallpaper, plates, cups, and ribbon) is available.

* *Garden,* outside, promotes understanding of science concepts, reading, and writing. I include pots, soil, seeds, small shovels, watering cans, and a center log, and pencils.

Orientation Day Activities

Routines and Rules

I teach in a school where we are given orientation days with the students. Our orientation days take place during the first week of school. The students come to school in small groups of four or five and stay for the entire day.

These orientation days are beneficial to both the students and the teachers. With only a few students in class on these days, the students are generally more at ease and adjust more quickly to the new environment and situation. In addition, the teacher is given the opportunity to work closely with each student and gets to know each individually. Our request for these invaluable days was granted with the support of our principal. Teachers who do not have these days can still accomplish the same goals with the entire class. However, realistically, it will require more time to get in touch with each student.

For five days, students come in small orientation groups of four or five. On these days, parents are welcome to walk around the room with their children to help them get oriented to the new environment. Then, when everyone has arrived, I ask the parents to say their good-byes. After they leave, I find that sharing a book is calming and comforting for the students. I usually select books about the first day of school. These stories help the students realize that many others share the same feelings they are experiencing. *Franklin Goes to School* (Bourgeois 1995), *Timothy Goes to School* (Wells 1981), or *Time for School, Nathan!* (Delacre 1989) are a few possible choices.

I go through a few routine procedures with the students: pledge of allegiance to the flag, attendance, and lunch count. We go through these routines very slowly so that the students will feel comfortable participating.

We read and discuss the rules chart together, allowing for a common ground for respect and behavior. These are the rules in my classroom:

Class Rules

Because we are friends and we care about each other we will . . .

1. Listen to others when others are speaking
2. Raise our hands when we want to share with our teacher or friends
3. Walk in the classroom, in the hallways, and on the sidewalks
4. Use a classroom voice and always try to do our best
5. Be careful not to hurt others

I take the students on an orientation walk around the school grounds. This helps them recognize that they are a part of a larger community known as their school. We meet "school helpers" such as the principal, the vice principal, office staff, the health room nurse, the counselor, the librarian, cafeteria workers, custodians, and other teachers, to help familiarize the students with the people who are there to help.

Reading Folders

The reading folder is a folder or composition book that contains a growing collection of rhymes, poems, and songs. On this first day of school, I select the familiar nursery rhyme "Humpty Dumpty." Each student receives a copy of the rhyme for his or her folder. Before reading, we look at the rhyme and see if there are any words or letters that are recognized. I ask the students to draw a picture of Humpty Dumpty or anything else that reminds them of this rhyme.

Drawing, Cutting, and Gluing

I cannot assume that the students have had experience using crayons, scissors, and glue. I find that if I spend time at the beginning of the year on the use of scissors and glue, it makes everything much easier throughout the year. On the first day of school, I use Humpty Dumpty as a means to cover these skills. I give each student two pieces of paper: one 6″ × 9″ piece to draw a brick or stone wall, and one 9″ × 12″ piece onto which the smaller piece is to be glued. They draw Humpty Dumpty on a separate sheet, cut out the picture of Humpty Dumpty, and glue it onto the brick wall. (The "fall" is accomplished by rotating the smaller piece downwards.) The students then write their names on the back. During this activity, I can see what skills they already have and introduce them to those they don't.

Writing Books or Journals

On this first day of school, I ask the students to write a story in their unlined composition book about anything that interests them. This first day usually produces lots of picture stories and maybe a name or two. The students "read" me their stories, and I write what they say on the page. While they are drawing their pictures some say, "I don't know how to write." To that I respond, "Sure, you do. You're writing right now." Once they know they cannot be "wrong" if they are writing their ideas, they want to write and write.

Calendar Activities

My students gather on the floor for the daily calendar activities. We begin by reading the days and dates for yesterday, today, and tomorrow. The first tally mark is placed on the tally chart; one tally will be added per day matching the date of the month. For example, August 9 would have nine tally marks. I use a large class book to write the date and an event occurring that day. The following is an example of what is written on a page of the class calendar book.

Today is Monday.

August 9, 1998.

8–9–98

We are going to the computer lab this morning.

As the year progresses, we add

Yesterday was Sunday.

Tomorrow will be Tuesday.

I model these calendar activities for the first few weeks, after which a weekly class leader is selected (this is rotated). Our class leaders may request help from the other students or myself, but soon they are writing information on the calendar themselves.

Friendship and Sharing

Friendship is an important concept to cover on the first day of school. There are many books related to friendship. I use books such as *May I Bring a Friend?* (De Regniers 1964), *Frog in the Middle* (Gretz 1991), and *Will I Have a Friend?* (Cohen 1967), and teach songs such as "Make New Friends," "The More We Get Together," and "Friendship Train," by Jim Valley.

Writing

The students write in their journals. Journal writing is a way for them to learn to use the written language to communicate with others. As this is new for most of the students, I want them to feel comfortable and excited about

Kim asks for her fellow students' suggestions on what to write on the daily calendar.

writing. I give them their blank books and encourage them to write anything they would like to include.

I like to have a sample of their beginning writing, drawing, and hand-writing, so I give them a piece of paper labeled "Self-Portrait." They write name and date on this paper and draw a picture of themselves. I have them do this again at the end of the year to demonstrate their progress and development over the school year. It always amazes me to see their developmental progress from August through June.

Reading

Mr. Grump (Cowley 1989) is a favorite with my students. I introduce this book in Big Book form. They listen to the story as I read it aloud. By the second reading, they are all chiming in on the repetitious parts. By the third reading, I point to the words and show the students the one-to-one correspondence between the spoken and written word.

Centers

There are so many centers that the students are eager to explore. I find that it is much more manageable to open only a few centers on the first day, usually blocks, puzzles, building toys, the library, and the Writing Center. This way the students have a variety from which to choose but not so many as to be overwhelmed.

Homework

I set aside the end of the first day for the students to borrow books for homework. Each of them borrows a book every day either to read to the family or to be read to by someone at home. I have tried many systems of checking out books and have found that pocketing each book with a card is the fastest way. In the beginning, it takes a great deal of time to pocket all the books, but you only have to do it once. Then, a student only needs to remove the card from the book and put it into the pocket chart by his or her name. The next morning the card is replaced into the book pocket.

I always remember to take it slowly and listen to the students during those hectic first few days of school. What I did last year may not be appro-

Austin and Joleen construct a block city in the Blocks Center.

priate for this year. I know that each class is different, with different interests and needs.

ALL STUDENTS SHOULD FIND enjoyment and success in learning. Because each student has an individual style of learning, a personal set of interests, and unique prior knowledge and experience, my expectation is that each will work to the best of her or his ability yet achieve varying results. Keeping in mind the wide range of interests and abilities, I provide diverse opportunities for learning in my classroom. I believe that all classrooms should provide an environment filled with written language. The next chapters share my teaching philosophy and the content and procedures involved in developing the curriculum.

Reading

I GLANCE UP AT THE CLOCK. A few minutes until recess. "Book Talks," I announce. I turn to the sign-up sheet and see that it is Laura and Mark's turn. Laura decides she wants to read a story from her writing book. She makes her selection and begins reading. "This is my dream house. It's a really nice house. I have my own room and my own closet. I am very excited about my dream house." She will be moving soon and has been listening to her family plan the move. The students listen with curiosity and eagerly ask questions about her new home. She shows them her drawing, a layout of her dream house. "It has an upstairs," she informs the others. "Do you get to sleep upstairs?" the students wonder. "My bedroom is at the top of the stairs. I am going to have a fish bathroom. My grandpa and grandma bought me a new shower curtain with fish on it." "Ohhh, that's cool," they all agree. They applaud in earnest at the end of her Book Talk. Mark is next. He has decided to read the predictable book *My Pocket* (Ditzel 1992a), which he borrowed to take home yesterday. He reads each page carefully. "Don't forget to show us the pictures," Krista says. Before turning the page, Mark turns the book around so all can see the pictures. When he finishes the book, the students begin to share some of their connections to the book. "I went to the beach last week and my sister found coral." "When I went to the beach, I caught a sand crab. It pinched me but it didn't hurt." "My grandpa took me to the beach. We went fishing. I caught lots and lots of fish." The students enthusiastically clap as the discussion finishes. The bell rings, and they prepare for recess. As they leave, I notice Claire, Max, and Cori are inspired to stop and sign up for Book Talks. Eager readers and learners. What a great morning!

This is the ultimate goal of my reading program—to see avid readers, able to respond to each other, confident of the choices they make. Reaching this point requires that I have a clear sense of my expectations for the whole class and a consistent practice that is grounded in current theories about reading instruction. What follows is a description of some of the principles and practices of my reading instruction.

Reading Aloud

Ideally, children should have been read to since birth. However, since I cannot make that assumption, I must expose my students to a variety of read-alouds every day. In addition to literature books, students love listening to chapter books. Some of their favorites include *Charlotte's Web* (White 1952) and *Freckle Juice* (Blume 1971). There are so many books to select from these days. I look for classics as well as new titles.

When I select a book to read aloud, it is sometimes related to a topic we are currently studying in class. For example, if we are covering insects, I would read *The Very Hungry Caterpillar* (1983) or *The Grouchy Ladybug* (1977), both by Eric Carle. Another way I select books may be to focus on a particular author. The students look for similarities and patterns in the writing and illustrations.

As an alternative to reading aloud prose, I read poetry. I select an anthology or a book of classic poems like *Favorite Poems, Old and New* (Ferris 1957), nature poems like *Creatures of Earth, Sea, and Sky* (Heard 1992), humorous poems like *The New Kid on the Block* (Prelutsky 1984), or a Mother Goose collection. The students always enjoy them. They seem to enjoy the rhythm and flow of the poetry. Their heads move up and down as I read, indicating their interest in and enjoyment of the words.

Using Big Books

I find Big Books to be a great way of having my students read together. When I use Big Books, all the students can see the words in the book and can participate in reading together. At first, I found using a Big Book to be tricky and awkward. I found that it really helped me to have an easel to hold up the book. I introduce the book by having the students read the title and predict the story content through the title and cover illustration. Then I point to the words as my class and I read aloud together. The students follow along and become aware of the one-to-one correspondence between spoken and written language.

I find Big Books helpful in the reading technique of predicting text. One method I find effective is to cover a word with a piece of paper. I ask the students to predict which words make sense in that context. The students skip the word and continue reading to the end of the sentence or passage. When I expose the first letter of the unknown word, more predictions are made using graphophonetic cues.

Big Book stories can be used as a base for extensions and innovations. Many of the stories have predictable texts that have a natural appeal to the students in creating extensions stemming from the original text. An example of this could be shown using *I Can Jump* (Cowley 1986). The text is as follows:

> "I can jump," said the grasshopper. "I can't jump," said the snail.
> "I can run," said the spider. "I can't run," said the snail.
> "I can fly," said the butterfly. "I can't fly," said the snail.
> "But I can slide."

An extension of this story would be to have the students rewrite the story while thinking of their own creatures and movements. For instance, they might write, "'I can swim,' said the fish, or 'I can leap,' said the frog."

Although I rarely do extensions and innovations, because I want the students to make their own choices about what to write, there are times when the students themselves initiate innovations from stories shared in class through a Big Book.

Looking for Reading Clues and Cues

Reading aloud helps students become familiar with written language. Listening to stories will allow them to hear the structure, rhythmic flow, and characteristics associated with the written language. Having been exposed to written language, they will be more comfortable reading themselves.

When the students are reading, I look to find which students understand a one-to-one correspondence between the written and spoken language. I can observe them as they are reading in groups or independently.

There are different cueing systems that will assist the students in reading new words. Successful readers realize that reading is obtaining meaning from the text. The cueing systems are used interchangeably and unconsciously as each system becomes necessary for a reader to function. Semantic cues are cues used in context to make sense of the passage, syntactic cues are the grammar and structure, and graphophonic cues are the sound/symbol relationships needed to help identify whether a word looks and sounds "right." All of these cueing systems are employed to derive meaning. Phonics alone does not necessarily promote full comprehension. Rather, it is an integral part of the reading process and used in conjunction with the other systems.

Picture Clues

Attending to picture clues is a natural first step in reading unfamiliar words. Pictures help to connect the text to the meaning. Readers will continually check back to the pictures for confirmation even when they are better readers. As they become more accomplished as readers, less time will be spent using this strategy. Picture reading then takes on a new form. It is used for inferring or predicting and for prompting discussion in groups.

Context Clues

A student's familiarity with written language will be of great benefit when using context clues. When students can hear the "rightness" in written language, they will be able to detect which words fit into the context of a passage. The use of known words before and after an unfamiliar word helps the reader decide what makes sense in that context. Students are taught to skip the unknown word, read on, then go back and see what possible words make sense.

Phonetic Clues

"Sounding out" a word basically means the reader is using phonetic clues to read an unknown word. A reader will generally start with the initial

Joleen, Taylor, and Lauren read a story during center time.

consonant, then attempt to use the context to determine the word. Sometimes readers will look for familiar word patterns, such as *ar*. Lindsey proudly explained that she sounded out *market:* "I said the *m*, then I said the *ar*. I knew it was *market* because that's where they were going in the story." In this example, Lindsey used phonetic clues as well as context and picture clues.

Constructing Meaning

Effective readers construct meaning while they read. They use preceding syntactic and semantic context to narrow the number of possible alternatives for the unfamiliar word. Prior knowledge and context are used to make these predictions.

Teacher Strategies During Reading

I use strategies to help the students predict and think when reading. I encourage them to self-correct by my prompting. When one of the students comes upon an unknown word while reading, it is very important that she know the different strategies to use to attack the word. Initially, I make the following suggestions when a student is unfamiliar with a word:

How can the picture help you?

Try skipping the word and finish reading the sentence or paragraph.

What word could fit here?

How does the word begin?

Does it make sense? Does it sound right?

Are there other words that begin the same way that make sense?

Are there parts of the word that look familiar to you?

Does that word make sense?

Reread the sentence. Does it sound right?

What did you do to read the unknown word?

Working with the Individual

I believe that the students need to feel positive about reading and to know that they can read. By having them read individually, I am encouraging them to be independent readers. To grow and improve as independent readers, the students need to be aware of what reading strategies are available to them and the ones they are already utilizing. They also need to be aware that sometimes one strategy is more effective than another for a given situation. As students become more fluent, they are able to determine which strategy is best for a given situation. Examples of encouragement and reinforcement I may use to make them aware of which reading strategies they are using are

"Wow, you read that book all by yourself."

"Great. I saw you look at the pictures to help you."

"I noticed you used different reading strategies."

"Good idea. I saw you skip this word and later go back and figure it out."

 ## Time Management

I find it very difficult to listen to twenty-five individual students reading to me daily. There just isn't enough time. However, there are several arrangements I use to alleviate this problem:

* The students choose a partner and take turns reading their books to each other. I walk around and listen, taking notes or encouraging as needed.

* Only one half or one fourth of the students read to me daily. The others can do partner reading.

* Students read to me intermittently during the day between activities. They don't all have to read at one specific time.

* Some students give Book Talks. Four or five students can read their books to the class.

* The students break into groups of four or five. They can read to each other in these small groups.

 ## Chalkboard Stories

Several times a week I write a story on the chalkboard. These stories contain words that are familiar to my students as well as words that are unknown. I leave a blank space within the story replacing one of the words. I call this the "mm" word. The students begin by reading all the words they recognize. Then we read the entire story skipping the unknown word in the blank space. After the students complete the passage, they predict what word makes sense in the "mm" space. I write in the first letter of the word and the

Claire can read our chalkboard story.

students make their predictions again. Sometimes I write in the suffix or last letter instead of the first letter. While predictions are being made, I ask the students, "Does that word make sense in this blank?" I teach and use reading strategies such as phonics, sight vocabulary (high-frequency words immediately recognized, such as *the* and *of*), decoding, predicting, and context cues through these lessons.

For example, while we were studying the life cycles of plants, I wrote this story on the board for the students to read.

> Yesterday we planted seeds. We need to take good care of them so they will grow
> _____. What will our seeds need?

I began by having the students read the words they knew. They were unfamiliar with the word *seeds.* I knew that *see* was a sight vocabulary word for the students, so I helped them decipher the word by first covering the letters *ds.* This way they were able to recognize the word *see.* Next, I exposed the letters *ds,* and the students used their knowledge of phonics to sound out the word. *Planted* was also unfamiliar to the students, but they were able to use their understanding of word parts to figure it out. First they said "pl" followed by "ant," then concluded that the word was *planted* because it had an "ed" at the end. Then the students read the story to me, saying "mm" when they came upon the blank. They predicted what words would make sense in the blank. They guessed many words, including *big, tall, green, strong, nice, leaves, fast,* and *quickly*. I wrote the letter *t* in the front of the blank, and they all chimed in "tall."

 ## Book Talks

I use Book Talks as a means by which the students are able to present a book or story they have read or written by sharing its highlights or actually reading the selection. During this time, main idea or summary skills are incorporated. Book Talks are very popular with the students. They enjoy getting up in front of the class and sharing with the others. I have a sign-up sheet from which I am able to call upon someone for a Book Talk any time of the day. Students choose to share books they have read at home, books they have heard in a read-aloud, or stories from their journals. This gives them opportunities to share with others new ideas and literature.

 ## The Reading Game

Many years ago, I found myself struggling to keep on listening to the students read their predictable "I Can Read" homework books. At that time, I knew I would have to come up with something more practical and interesting. That's when the Reading Game developed. Each student comes back to school with the book he has read for homework. I have him select a partner, find a place in the room, and "teach" his book to his partner. After teaching their books to each other, the pair trades books and comes to the waiting area, consisting of two chairs in the front of the room. Here they wait for new partners. Each returning child selects a new partner and the process repeats. When new partners are chosen, the two pairs go off and teach their books to their new partners, and the cycle continues. Meanwhile, I circulate around the classroom, listening, observing, and taking note of the students' reading. We do this for about ten to fifteen minutes. That's just enough time for me to get around. This game takes place once a month or so. I try to vary the activities so that neither the students nor I get bored.

Literature Circles

In *Creating Classrooms for Authors* (1988) Harste, Short, and Burke discuss the value of using Literature Circles in the classroom. The purpose of Literature Circles is to extend the meaning that a reader has gained from a book or to explore new meaning by talking about the book with others. I explain to the parents of my students that it works the same way as talking about a movie with a friend. You leave the movie with your own interpretation and understanding. By talking about it with a friend, you are able to think more critically and deepen your understanding. The interpretations we create are based on our personal experiences. Therefore, different meanings can evolve from the same movie. When participating in a Literature Circle, readers are able to expand their thinking and see varying points of view.

I begin Literature Circles with the whole class using one book. We read and discuss the book. I usually start with a basic question such as "What was this story about?" As they talk about the book, I am able to see what parts are of interest to them. We focus on those parts and make connections from the book to their own experiences. This helps to deepen their understanding.

Once I feel the students understand how Literature Circles work, we try them in small groups. I like to use literature books from text sets. The text set can be around any theme. After a Book Talk on each book, the students sign up for one of the books that they would like to explore further. I usually have three selections (see the color insert).

The first group begins by predicting the story through the cover and title. We have a discussion following the reading of the book, just as I did with the whole class. The purpose is the same: to make connections to life experiences and to extend meaning and interpretation. Our discussion may last over several days. The participants of this Literature Circle present the book to the rest of the class. Songs, puppet shows, dramatics, stories, and plays are just a few of the ways that the students have chosen to share. I need to allow the students to make the decisions when sharing their explorations into the literature.

I find that I can work with three groups if the starting times are

staggered. When one group has finished discussing or is planning its presen-
tation, I can begin working with the next group.

Creating a Reading-Rich Environment

It takes a lot of organization to make sure the classroom is inviting for young
readers. I wish someone had told me as a young teacher exactly what I
needed to have in my classroom for reading. Before I even open up a book
and begin reading aloud, I've put a lot of time into creating spaces in my
room that encourage children to read. I've developed procedures that provide comfortable reading routines. I want to close this chapter with some
practical information about what materials and procedures have worked
best for me in helping young readers develop their reading skills.

Labeling

Labeling objects in the classroom offers an opportunity for the students to
be exposed to written language. Some teachers may decide to label objects in
the classroom before the start of the school year. I label the room together
with the students at the beginning of the year because there may be objects
that they would choose to label that I wouldn't have selected. Items we might
label are the map, globe, door, television, books, sink, computer, aquarium,
and chalkboard. Everything and anything can be labeled.

Charts

In my classroom, I employ many, many charts: charts sharing information,
charts containing frequently used words, charts of poems and rhymes. The
charts are readily available for the students to use as a reference or to obtain
a word for their writing. Sometimes the students just want to go over with a
pointer and sing a song or recite a poem.

   One important chart is titled "Reading Strategies." Each year, after I
have taught different reading strategies to the class, the students come up
with this chart. The chart lists reading strategies that they may use when

These children are finding a word on a song chart to use in their writing.

they are unfamiliar with a word. The following is an example from my students:

Reading Strategies

Look at the picture.

Look at the first letter of the word you don't know.

Look at the ending of the word.

Look to see if the word looks like another word that you know.

Skip the word, read some more, then come back and see what word might fit.

Ask yourself if the word makes sense in the sentence.

Ask someone what the word says.

Always check if it fits and makes sense.

Reading Folders

In my classroom, we use reading folders that are portfolios or books containing copies of songs, rhymes, and poems I have taught to the students. The format can be anything that will accommodate these copies. The purpose of the reading folders is to promote reading through familiar and catchy jingles. When teaching a song, rhyme, or poem, I first write it on a piece of chart paper. This way all the students are able to see the text as we read it together. We first locate words we recognize, then using various reading strategies, we decipher the unknown words. I give each student a copy to be put into her book or portfolio. It is important that all the students keep their pages in proper order for future reference. These reading folders are brought out any time for singing or for use as a dictionary to find a word.

Text Sets

When we read, we are able to understand the content by bringing in our past experiences to make sense of the text. Past experiences may be an event or activity that we have seen or participated in. It also includes experiences with books we have read or even written.

Text sets are sets of books and other reading materials that are related by a common thread. I use these text set materials:

Leo Lionni

> *Alexander and the Wind-up Mouse* (1969)
>
> *Frederick* (1967)
>
> *Swimmy* (1963)
>
> *Biggest House in the World* (1968)
>
> *Inch by Inch* (1960)

Ocean Animals

> *Swimmy* (Lionni 1963)
>
> *Dolphins* (Cousteau Society 1991a)
>
> *Whales* (Cousteau Society 1992)
>
> *Fish Is Fish* (Lionni 1970)
>
> *National Geographic* magazines

We have many author text sets in the Library Center.

The Three Little Pigs

> *The Three Little Pigs* (Marshall 1989)
>
> *The Three Little Wolves and the Big Bad Pig* (Trivizas 1993)
>
> *The True Story of the Three Little Pigs! By A. Wolf* (Scieszka 1989)
>
> *The Fourth Little Pig* (Celsi 1992)
>
> *The Three Little Javelinas* (Lowell 1992)

Other Text Sets

> Caldecott Award books
>
> Fairy tales
>
> Illustrations
>
> Friendship
>
> Topics of interest to the children

I find that when reading materials are grouped into text sets, the students are encouraged to extend their understanding of the texts because of previous experiences with other related books from the text set. Text sets are ideal for Literature Circle selections.

As I have mentioned, text sets contain reading materials that are related by theme, topic, event, author, and so on. They can contain books, magazines, songs, poems, and newspaper articles. In kindergarten, these text sets may be read with the entire class or by smaller Literature Circle groups.

Library Center

The Library Center contains a wide range of reading materials from my collection as well as high-interest books I have borrowed from the school and public libraries. I have magazines and newspapers because they are interesting to read and are used as a reference by the students. I always scan these first to avoid content and subjects that I feel are objectionable and inappropriate for my students. Books in this center can be arranged or categorized in any way that is logical to the students. In my Library Center, books are housed in plastic containers. I keep all of the Birthday Books together so that my students can easily find the books they brought in. Books dealing with plants, animals, and insects are grouped in their own separate containers. I find that we are all able to locate books easily with this system. In addition, books are separated into containers by the students' favorite authors, for example,

Aliki

Jan Brett

Marc Brown

Eve Bunting

Eric Carle

Tomie de Paola

Mem Fox

Jack Gantos

Ezra Jack Keats

Leo Lionni

Bill Martin, Jr.

Mercer Mayer

Raffi

H. A. Rey

Audrey and Don Wood

I share this quotation with the students' parents when I talk with them about reading (it was given to me without its original source): "A love of literature is developed through the fun of being involved with a variety of quality printed materials." This quotation captures the goal of my reading program. I want students to love books, and everything I do as a teacher in organizing the classroom and instructing students is an attempt to foster joy in reading.

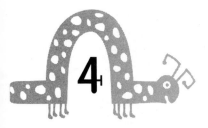

Writing

ON MY CLASSROOM WALL I have a quotation from Frank Smith: "There is no point in learning to spell if you have no intention of writing." I think that says it all.

We begin writing on the first day of school. I encourage my students to write their ideas and stories in their journals. They are given unlined composition books for journal writing. At this point, I believe that lines only restrict the students' writing. Too much attention is given to staying within the lines rather than to expressing ideas.

Initially, most of the students draw pictures. After a week or two, when they are comfortable recording their ideas, I begin my first writing lesson. I take out my two copies of *Do You Want to Be My Friend?* (Carle 1971). After sharing the wordless version, I bring out the version with words. When comparing the two versions, the students immediately point out that one is wordless and one has words. I then tell them that I would like their stories to contain words, too. From that point, they include a written story along with the pictures.

As the year progresses, the picture writing gives way to more written language. Written stories usually begin with random letters. Eventually, the random letters give way to initial consonants or word parts. As the students write daily, conventional spelling develops. Our classroom is covered with written language. The students will turn to a chart, a book, or a label in the room if it contains a word they need for their story. The students know they may ask someone for help in finding or writing a word. I encourage them to

Amelia and Michellei are writing stories in their journals.

remember short words like *at* to aid them in spelling words containing *at* (*bat, cat, fat, mat*).

At the beginning, many of the students will ask me how to spell words. I usually respond by saying, "Say the word slowly. What letters do you hear in the word?" Even though they may say letters that are not in the word, I still encourage them to write it. They become more confident in writing and eventually won't be overly concerned with spelling but focus on the ideas.

The students may choose to continue writing a story already in progress or make a new entry in their journals. I ask that they write the date on the top of each entry so that I can see their progress throughout the year. They may want to read their stories to others in class. I find that Book Talks are a great way to share stories. One of my early writing lessons helps the students broaden their story ideas. We work on a chart like the following, composed by the students:

Where Do Writers Get Their Ideas?

1. Think in their heads

2. Read another book and get an idea

3. TV shows

4. Movies

5. A place you visited

6. Something that happened to you

7. Talking to someone

8. Watching people

Inventive or Temporary Spelling

Inventive or temporary spelling allows the students to focus on writing ideas. This is the primary advantage of inventive spelling. Allowing its use frees them to write and share thoughts and ideas without having to stop the writing flow to ask how to spell a word. Rather, they use the information they already know and apply it in their writing. This information might include left to right directionality or the understanding that letters make up printed resources around our room, such as books, charts, and labels. When my students come to a word they don't know how to spell, they are confident and independent in their writing and can use different writing strategies.

I demonstrate how to use inventive spelling on the chalkboard with the class. First, we decide what we want to write. Then together we sound the words out slowly one at a time. The students tell me the letters they hear, and I write them down. We do this lesson many times at the beginning of the school year.

I demonstrate to the students how they can use printed material around the room to help in their spelling. I might ask, "If you need to spell the word *like,* where could you look to find it?" They may show me a book or a chart containing that word. Then I might say, "Good, if you see a word that you need, take it."

I explain inventive spelling to the students' parents so that they can be involved with their child's writing at home. I find that taking the time to explain inventive spelling allows parents to help reinforce writing at home.

Their biggest concern is their belief that by allowing students to use inventive spelling, poor spellers are being created. I have found that when students write daily and really want to write, conventional spelling develops. The students use inventive spelling to get their ideas down on paper. In addition to being surrounded by print in my classroom, they are continually exposed to and taught conventional spelling. They are encouraged to use conventional spelling throughout the year in their writing, but allowing inventive spelling at first lets them enjoy writing. Sharing the *Reading and Writing at Home* booklet (see Appendix C) with parents gives them the opportunity to set up environments at home that promote reading and writing.

I encourage the students to focus on their ideas so they will be comfortable writing independently. On Austin's first day in kindergarten he drew a picture and dictated this story: "I went rollerblading." Toward the end of the school year his stories clearly had his "voice" and ideas. In May, he wrote, "I like *Star Wars*. It was a fun movie. I can never stop talking about it. Did you like it, too?"

Austin's rollerblading drawing on the first day of school.

Austin's Star Wars *story in May.*

Writing Activities

Center Logs

Center logs are blank books kept in areas such as the Science Center. In my classroom, we use these logs to keep track of an experiment or to keep records of activities occurring in that center. It is a great way for students to communicate with each other or with me. The students are encouraged to write questions and observations in the form of pictures or words in these logs. Other students and I respond to the entries. I always ask the students to write their names on each entry in case there are any questions.

Writing Center

Writing Center contains all the materials needed to communicate through writing: paper, pens, pencils, envelopes, stickers, a mailbox, a message board, and a list of students' and teachers' names with photos. I encourage the students to write short messages to each other. They write a message, fold it, write the name of the recipient on the outside of the message, then tack it to the message board. Some choose to write a letter, put it into an envelope, write the name of the sender and recipient, place a sticker for a stamp, and mail it in the classroom mailbox. These are just a few ways I encourage written communication.

Publishing Books

Book publishing takes the writer from an idea through the writing process. The students start with an idea. After gathering their thoughts on paper, they share the writing with another person. They may choose to edit their stories if there are questions or suggestions. Next, they bring their work to the editor, me. We work together, editing spelling and grammar as needed. After revisions are made, the stories are ready to be put into book form.

The students determine how their stories are to be structured and where the page breaks are to go. They decide on an exciting title, a dedication page, and an About the Author page. They then print their stories on the computer. I teach them how to bind their books by sewing the pages together. After illustrating their books, the students produce covers for them. In my classroom, the students make covers using cloth and oaktag for durability. The completed books are read to other classes. This allows for a publication celebration. My kindergarten students are always excited to go through the publishing process.

Newspaper

The publication of a class newspaper gives the students another form of writing experience. News reports and editorials provide opportunities to write accurate and factual information. The students need to go through this writing process as they would with any other type of writing. The newspaper is set up in six sections. "Local News" reports events occurring in our classroom and the school community. "Sports" reports activities in our community related to athletic events. Some even write about sporting events seen on television. "Book Reviews" reports on favorite and popular books selected by the reporter. In the section "Family Stories," students may publish writing done at home with their families, either fictional or based upon interviews by the students. The "Personal Column" is open for the students to write letters to others. The letters vary and include messages, questions, and opinions. The last section, "Editorials," is for the students to write what their feelings are about school. Newspaper writing differs from journal and story writing. I know that experience with these various styles of writing can only enhance the students' learning about writing.

Handwriting

Handwriting was emphasized in school when I was growing up. From my personal experience as a student, I know my fine motor skills were and, for the most part, still are not the best. Fortunately, computers and word processors were invented.

I believe that penmanship does need to be legible; for instance, it is important that a pharmacist be able to read a handwritten prescription. However, as long as handwriting is legible (if not beautiful), I feel it is acceptable as a tool for written communication. I believe that the greater emphasis should be on the content and enjoyment of writing. The purpose of handwriting is only to communicate what is written. When students are given handwriting drills, they become a tedious chore for most. We all tend to write less if we don't enjoy writing.

Parents always ask me if I teach formal handwriting. My response is that I do demonstrate and model the conventional formation of letters and encourage the students to apply it in their writing. I do not expect perfect penmanship and do not feel the need for repeated tracing and board copying. My primary purpose is to have the students love writing and to feel good about themselves as writers. The more you write, the better the writer you become.

Math, Science, and Social Studies

STUDENT- AND TEACHER-INITIATED curriculum within the content areas of math, science, and social studies are the center of our studies. Reading and writing are the modes in which to acquire, reflect on, and make sense of the content.

Learning through inquiry focuses on each individual student. It builds on students' prior knowledge, their background experiences, encourages them to work collaboratively, learn from peers, and gives them an active part in determining the curriculum in varying subject areas.

In what follows, I describe some of the ways I teach math, science, and social studies throughout the year.

Math

It's the sixteenth day of the month. My students are working in pairs, forming different arrays and equations using cubes. Lauren and Chase call out, "We made an array 1 by 16." Austin and Elliott have made one that is 2 by 8 and decide that $8 + 8 = 16$. "Look, 16 is a square number! That's a big square number," exclaims Marcus as he shows me his 4 by 4 array. I think to myself that this would be the perfect time to read *One Hundred Hungry Ants* (Pinczes 1993). The students are intrigued as 100 ants in the story march in a single file, in two rows of 50, four rows of 25, five rows of 20, and finally ten rows of 10 forming a 10 by 10 array. "Ohhh, that's a really big square number!" Marcus says, making a connection to his array. The students tackle problems with multiple solutions and ways of solving. Lessons like these should emphasize and encourage reasoning, problem solving, and thinking.

Classification

I teach the concept of classification in the fall. During this time, pumpkins are readily available, and during one designated week each family sends in one pumpkin. The pumpkins come to school in various colors, shapes, sizes, and textures. The students use these pumpkins as manipulatives to sort, sequence, pattern, and measure. In addition, vocabulary development comes naturally. This activity is meaningful to the students because they are directly involved in making the decisions as to which attributes they use to classify. My students need to learn to sort objects by color, shape, size, or any other attribute. Initially, I introduce the concept of classification in a large group. I begin by sorting the students into groups of boys and girls. As the students discover how I am classifying the others, they are encouraged to join the group to which they belong. Other possibilities for sorting the students are by hair color, clothing attributes (color, buttons or zippers), footwear, and so on. Interest rises as they try to guess the basis for the classification and to include themselves in the proper group.

Then I ask each student to get an object from the classroom and put it in a circle. They watch as I sort the objects by color. After they decide how I sorted these objects, I try it with other attributes. Once the students understand the concept of classification, I give them boxes containing shells, small tiles, buttons, keys, colored pasta (see recipe in Appendix A), or anything else I have collected. They use these objects at their desks to sort. I like to have the students work with a partner at first, to build confidence.

Patterning

Patterning is the second math concept I teach my students. Patterning must follow classification because the students need to know which objects belong together before discovering patterns in them. This is an important concept to grasp early on because patterns are everywhere in mathematics. Again, I first present this concept in a large group, placing the students in a line pat-

Chase and Cori create their own patterns with pattern blocks.

tern of boy, girl, boy, girl. I give each student unifix cubes, ten each of two colors. I have them create the boy/girl pattern with the unifix cubes. Initially, an intuitive pattern like AB is created, but later more complex patterns such as ABB or AAB emerge. The students soon want to create more challenging patterns using three, four, or five colors. I continue to introduce patterning in a large group using manipulatives such as buttons, colored pasta, or any other collected objects. I ask the students to create patterns at their desks with a partner. A useful reference is *Mr. Noisy's Book of Patterns* (Williams 1995b), which extends patterning beyond objects. Once this concept has been introduced, the students notice and point out patterns everywhere we go. They notice patterns on the buildings, in nature, on their clothing, and even on book jackets. It becomes a concept covered throughout the day.

Numeration

The concept of numeration includes counting, numeral recognition, and one-to-one correspondence. I incorporate numeration into daily routines such as calendar activities and through literature books. *Anno's Counting Book* (Anno 1975b) and *The Skip Count Song* (Williams 1995c) are examples of books that I use to reinforce these concepts. The students use numeration in a wide variety of activities, including reading signs and books or fairly dividing objects during play.

Each fall I bring a pumpkin to school. We begin our inquiry with what the students already know and what questions they have about pumpkins. The students may make predictions as to how many pumpkin seeds they think are in the pumpkin by looking at its size. After opening the top, the students may want to make changes to their predictions. I have the students count the seeds putting them into portion cups containing ten seeds per cup. When all the seeds have been grouped, the students can count the number of seeds that were in the pumpkin and validate their predictions. This one lesson promotes predicting, validating, counting by ones, one-to-one correspondence, and counting by tens and possibly by hundreds. In addition, reading books about seeds, a discussion about other seeds people eat and what grows from each seed, and writing about or recording this information incorporates not only math but reading, writing, science, and social studies.

Graphing

Graphing is a way to visualize accumulated data or sets of numbers. I introduce graphing at the beginning of the year, starting with a concrete rather than an abstract graph. I read and discuss *Picking Apples and Pumpkins* (Hutchings and Hutchings 1994). I pass out small cups of apple juice, muffin cups of apple chips, and bowls of applesauce (see recipe in Appendix A). I ask the students to sample each. I have a large floor graph, made by drawing lines on an inexpensive shower curtain. At the baseline, I place apple juice, apple chips, and applesauce labels. I ask the students to select their favorite one and place their empty cups or bowls on the floor graph. Usually one category accumulates more utensils than the other two. We discuss what the graph is showing. I ask questions, such as which category was selected by more students, or how many chip/juice pairs were selected. I ask each student to draw her selection on a small piece of paper and replace the cup or bowl with the picture. We discuss how the information on the graph hasn't changed because the actual object has been replaced with a picture. Next, the students transfer their pictures onto a paper graph. Again, we discuss how the information on the graph hasn't changed, but they now have an abstract rather than a concrete graph. Graphing becomes meaningful as the students or I select graphing topics related to their interests.

Measurement

Measurement can be done using both standard and nonstandard units. I have the students trace their footprints. These footprints can be used as a unit of measure, as in *How Big Is a Foot?* (Myller 1962). Unifix cubes are another nonstandard unit that is simple to use because they lock together. Using nonstandard, concrete units of measure makes it easier for the students to grasp the concept of measurement. Using nonstandard units of measure allows them to concentrate on the concept of measurement and distance rather than on the exact dimensions of the unit of measure. Once they understand measurement, standard units of measure should be introduced. I let the students' parents know that I send home a Weekend Bag to reinforce this concept (see Chapter 6).

Shapes

I introduce two- and three-dimensional shapes during the year. I teach and reinforce the students' knowledge of shapes by using vocabulary such as *square, pyramid,* and *sphere* while referring to objects containing these shapes as well as to instructional wooden solids. Reading books with shape vocabulary is another form of reinforcement. The students are then able to use these vocabulary words while playing in the Blocks Center or describing objects.

Colors

I have found that most of my kindergartners enter school knowing the basic colors. I extend their vocabulary by introducing primary and secondary colors. I use *Mouse Paint* (Walsh 1989) with its bold illustrations as a way of introducing the mixing of colors. I provide a cookie sheet and squeeze bottles of paints in the primary colors. Each bottle is labeled with the color it contains. The students are able to mix their own colors on the cookie sheet to use for their paintings.

Time

Time is a concept that the students are always anxious to learn. I use *Clocks and More Clocks* (Hutchins 1970) and *The Time Song* (Williams 1995d) to help reinforce this concept. We play time games using a teacher demonstration clock and student clocks. The students are given a specified time and set their clocks accordingly. Several students are also at the chalkboard writing the time so that we can see what the time looks like in written form. This comes after several sessions of demonstration and modeling. The students become familiar with the long, short, and second hands, and should be able to tell time to the hour and half hour.

Money

Recognition of money and its value can be taught for a couple of minutes daily. I use a chart with pockets and some coins and ask the students to make coin combinations to match the date. For instance, on October 1, we would put 1 penny, or 1 cent, into the pocket chart. On October 16, we would put in 1 dime, 1 nickel, and 1 penny, and count "10, 15, 16." We would also show that there are other coin combinations that make 16, such as 3 nickels and 1 penny, which would be counted as "5, 10, 15, 16." There are many combinations that can be made as the date gets higher. Books such as *The Magic Money Box* (Williams 1995a) and *Let's Find Out About Money* (Barabas 1997) and poems such as "Smart" from *Where the Sidewalk Ends* (Silverstein 1974) help me reinforce the concept.

Place Value

Place value can also be taught for a couple of minutes in the morning. Using coffee stirrers or straws, I keep track of the number of days in kindergarten. I label three cups as "ones," "tens," and "hundreds." Each morning we add a straw to the "ones" cup. After ten days, the straws are bunched together with a rubber band and moved from the "ones" cup to the "tens" cup. We write the number alongside the place value cups, allowing the students to see how many straws are in the cups and to understand what each number represents, for instance, 23 means two tens and three ones.

Addition

Addition should be taught with the use of manipulatives. I find that little plastic tiles with magnets on the back work well for class demonstrations so that all the students can see the board. I teach addition according to the date.

For example, on October 1, one tile is placed on the magnetic board. Equations such as $1 + 0 = 1$ or $0 + 1 = 1$ can be shown using the tiles. On October 16, the tiles can be arranged into a 4 by 4 square, and square numbers can be introduced. Equations such as $16 + 0 = 16$, $4 + 4 + 4 + 4 = 16$, or $10 + 6 = 16$ can be shown with the tiles. This should be done for a few minutes on a daily basis. In the spring, the students can use tiles or wooden cubes at their desks. Working with a partner, they create their own equations based on the date. I like *One Hundred Hungry Ants* (1993) or *A Remainder of One* (1995), both by Elinor J. Pinczes, to reinforce the idea that numbers form arrays and can be counted and added within these groups. After reading these books, the students can create story problems using these numbered arrays.

Subtraction

Subtraction does not need to be taught too early in the year. Once the students understand the concept of addition, I find subtraction falls into place quite naturally. I use the same plastic tiles to teach subtraction as we used for addition. I use story problems created by the students as well as myself and base them on actual situations such as the daily attendance.

Inquiry in Science and Social Studies

Inquiry is a process. It is especially suitable as a method for teaching science and social studies. This process begins with the students' interests, experiences, and knowledge. Inquiry invites students to become active in determining the direction of their curriculum. The students can learn only by connecting new information to their background experiences and prior knowledge. It is essential to take the time to listen to the students. Listening to them allows me to gauge where to begin teaching a particular subject or lesson. It is vital for my classroom environment to be conducive to social learning because students are able to gain new perspectives and information by working collaboratively.

Inquiry means questioning. I begin content area study and research with the students' background and experiences. I think about science and social studies curriculum expectations for the year in kindergarten. To launch an inquiry with the class, I ask the students what they know about a particular subject. When I consider the students' questions in conjunction with what I want to cover, they are naturally more interested in looking for the answers. By focusing on what interests them, trust is built into this process. This trust is vital to the start of the students' taking ownership of their own learning. Also, the possibility of reteaching what they already understand is avoided.

I start an inquiry by having students think about what background knowledge they have and what they still need to learn. They begin by sharing all the information they already know. This information is written on a chart like the following:

What Do You Know About Bats?

Bats have wings.

They can fly.

They live in caves.

They are scary.

As the students share their ideas, one thought prompts others. I accept all ideas so that the students know that their contributions are important. The chart can always be revised as more information is gathered. I write each student's name next to his idea for future reference as well as to give him ownership.

Next, we create another chart with questions from the students:

What Do You Want to Know About Bats?

How come bats don't fly into the walls of the caves?

What do bats eat?

Where do they come from?

Are they birds?

Do they lay eggs?

Do they bite people?

When the students are done thinking of questions that make them wonder, I know where to begin the study or research. Rather than spending a lot of time introducing concepts and ideas that the students already know, I am able to concentrate on new, more thought-provoking information.

We gather newspaper articles, magazine stories, books, videotapes, and computer encyclopedia information, and go on related field trips to begin the researching process. We read and talk and write and talk some more. The students refer back to the chart of questions as a focus in their search for answers.

When all the data have been collected, we need to decide how to share this information with others. The students come up with different ways to present the information. They may decide to write a song incorporating the facts that were gathered. Sometimes they prefer dramatics such as a puppet show or play. Sometimes they choose to do an art project and write. Poetry, individual and group books, and murals are other forms in which the students have chosen to present information. The students all have different interests and strengths. They do best when they know they are trusted.

I vary the method of inquiry. I ask the students to select one of three topics to study. For instance, during October, bats, skeletons, and spiders fit in nicely. When my class was studying about the ocean, I let the students select three ideas within the topic of the ocean to study. Sometimes I work with a couple of other kindergarten teachers and classes. The students in three classes sign up for the topic they are most interested in researching. We mix the students from the different classes. Each teacher assists one group, and at the end of the research the groups present the information they obtained. It's a good way to cover a lot of content in a short time as well as to integrate the different content areas.

Science

Science is a good content area to study using the inquiry method. Although each individual school has an overall curriculum plan, areas of particular interest to the students should also be emphasized. For example, we have a unit based on the life cycles of insects. We begin this unit with the prior knowledge and background of the students.

A good place to start would be with the question "What do you know about insects?" The students give information such as "Some insects can fly" and "Insects have six legs." They are then able to share with and teach the others what they know about insects before even beginning the lessons. I then ask, "What do you want to know about insects?" The students may ask

Amelia and her mother on a bug hunt.

questions such as "Why do bees make honey?" or "Are spiders insects?" This gives them the opportunity to think of what questions might interest them within the topic of insects. We research and gather information from a variety of printed materials as well as through observation of different insects.

We extend this unit by inviting parents to a curriculum day during which they interact with their children in several activities. These activities include making a bug box or bug net, going on a bug hunt, observing insects and looking for specific characteristics, and creating representations of insects through a variety of art media. The unit ends with discussion and assessment: "What have you learned about insects?" The students are able to continue researching and observing insects at home. Sometimes, after the inquiry is complete, new inquiry focuses emerge from the questions that arose during our discussions and research. We may choose to continue with these new inquiries, or the students are free to continue on their own time.

Social Studies

Social studies concepts studied in kindergarten will vary according to the individual school's social studies plan. Many kindergarten classrooms start with an "All About Me" social studies unit.

I incorporate the inquiry method into the area of social studies just as I do with science. For example, we tie together National Geography Week and Thanksgiving by having our annual kindergarten tasting party feature foods from different countries. I read *Yoko* (Wells 1998) to my class. The students listen intently as Yoko and her friends have an International Food Day in which they sample foods from different cultures. "That's just like our class," Kienen exclaims. I ask the students, "What do you know about different people and cultures?" The students then share some of the knowledge and experience they have with different cultures. "My grandma speak Filipino to my grandpa" and "I eat kim chee every night for dinner" are comments shared. I then ask, "What do you want to know about different cultures?" Immediately questions arise, especially about different food and clothing. They ask, "What do people eat in Africa?" and "Why do people wear different kinds of clothes?" A perfect opportunity to pull down the map to locate and discuss various countries and regions. We research and seek answers to their questions. I read books such as *Chinese New Year* (Ditzel 1992c), *This Is the Way We Eat Our Lunch* (Baer 1995), *A Country Far Away* (Gray 1988), and *How My Parents Learned to Eat* (Friedman 1984) to give them an idea of cultural similarities and differences through literature. After the information gathering is over, I ask the students, "What have you learned about different cultures?" Once again, the inquiry may end, or new focuses may emerge.

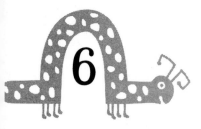

6

Parents as Partners

EVERY YEAR PARENTS ASK, "What can I do to help my child learn to read and write?" Parents are a terrific resource. Our job is to help them be active participants in their children's learning.

 ## Parent Orientation

We begin each year with a parent orientation. During our parent orientation, parents, guardians, and grandparents are invited to join the kindergarten teachers in the cafeteria for a read-aloud workshop (see outline in Appendix B). We emphasize reading aloud because we feel strongly that it is the key to building a strong base of family support at home.

After the read-aloud workshop, we hope our participants will

* Become more knowledgeable and comfortable about reading aloud— the selection of books and when, where, and how to read aloud

* Gain skills in reading aloud

* Be encouraged to commit themselves to reading aloud to the children

* Know how to select high-quality literature as well as books that interest their children

Parent Packet

I put together an informational packet to hand out at the parent orientation. The packet includes a Student Information Form and a booklet *Reading and Writing at Home* (see Appendix C) as well as some letters. The letters help me describe or explain various topics for the coming school year. One of the letters explains our Birthday Book tradition. I ask the parents to donate a hardcover or paperback book to our classroom library on their child's birthday. The students bring in a book with their photo and a bookplate naming them. This book remains in the classroom for the students to read and borrow. My former students have even come back years later looking for their Birthday Books. The parents agree that this is a wonderful way to celebrate their children's birthdays. I use the letter we developed together as kindergarten teachers:

Boys with their Birthday Books.

We are trying to make your child's birthday a meaningful one. How about letting your child treat our class to a Birthday Book on his or her birthday? The birthday child may bring a literature book (wrapped in birthday paper if you wish) that she or he would give to the class. This book would become a permanent part of our classroom library. You might want to include an individualized bookplate with your child's photo on the inside cover. What a special way for your child to share his or her birthday!

Thank you,
Kindergarten Teachers
P.S. You may see your child's teacher for a suggested book list.

 # Parental Involvement

Welcoming parents into our classroom and keeping them informed about the education of their children is very important. I believe we need to create a partnership between home and school. Trust and bonds with parents develop from open communication. Parents must realize that they are vital in their children's education. There are many ways in which I involve parents through participation at home as well as at school.

Most parents have busy schedules that do not allow for regular participation during the school day. I send home projects involving cutting or bookbinding. I also send home a wish list of "junk"—old keys, buttons, ribbons, wrapping paper, shells. I ask parents to collect such objects for us. These are used for art or as math manipulatives.

Some parents, however, do not work outside the home, or they have flexible schedules and are able to come into the classroom during the day. Their involvement does not have to be limited to photocopying, tutoring, or chaperoning field trips. I have developed a mini-program called Parents as Teachers. This program utilizes the resources of our parents to benefit our students.

Parents are encouraged to teach mini-lessons to the class. The lessons vary, depending on the topics the parents are comfortable teaching about. For example, the students named one mother our "mad scientist." She taught lessons on mold, air pressure, static electricity, and similar science topics of interest to the students. Another parent was our "nurse" and taught lessons about the heart, the pulse, and feelings.

Parents as Teachers gives the parent volunteers the opportunity to prepare lessons and gather materials. They present and discuss a problem with the students. They leave the problem at a special center for the students to observe during the week. For example, the students may predict where mold will grow fastest or observe celery slowly becoming blue in blue water. The parents return the following week to discuss what the children have observed and to present a new problem. I feel that all parents have much to offer and should be given the trust, responsibility, and opportunity to contribute.

Most parents love reading to the students. I have parent readers who come once a week to read aloud to the students. These parents are aware of the students' interests and select books accordingly. After each reading session, they ask the students what books or types of books they would like to have brought in the following week.

All parents want to be kept informed about the things we do in school.

Kim and her mother discover a variety of insects hiding under a cone.

When I have something to share with them, I send home newsletters. My newsletters go home filled with interesting, useful, and timely information. Some are about units we are working on at the time and the purpose for doing them. Some thank the students for Birthday Books or thank people who have volunteered. I believe that when parents see these newsletters they are encouraged to participate and become more actively involved. It is important to communicate your teaching philosophy to parents. I explain that critical thinking and problem solving should be encouraged with the students. I let parents know that I want the students to be risk takers anxious to seek information and use knowledge actively.

 # Homework

Two different types of books are sent home for homework. These books are sent home daily and are expected back the next morning.

The first type is the "I Can Read" books. Basically, they are predictable books to be read by the child to the parent. These predictable books have short, simple, catchy texts that can be learned easily by the children. *The Farm Concert* (Cowley 1983) is an example of an "I Can Read" book. After hearing the story a couple of times, the children are able to read it back to the parents.

The second type is the "Read to Me" books. These are literature books to be read to the child by the parent. There are so many high-quality literature books available these days. I find that some good sources of "Read to Me" books are book clubs, book sales, or the Birthday Book program.

I prepare homework envelopes to help ensure that books get home and back safely. I utilize two kinds of envelopes. The first kind of envelope is marked I Can Read and is used to transport predictable books such as *Mrs. Wishy-Washy* (Cowley 1980). On one side of the envelope are directions for completing the assignment and on the other side is the reading log, where information about the books is recorded.

The second kind of envelope is marked Read to Me and is used to transport read-aloud literature books. Again, on one side of the envelope are directions and on the other side is the reading log. I explain the Read to Me program in a letter to parents:

Reading Log

Date	Title	Comments

Reading log on homework envelope.

Dear Parents,

The single most important activity for building the knowledge required for success in reading is reading aloud to children. For this reason, I will be reading a variety of entertaining and stimulating books to the children throughout the school year. Parents play an important role in laying the foundation for learning to read, too. To further build our partnership in educating your child, I am starting a Read to Me program.

The purposes of the program are to

1. Help your child enjoy books and want to learn to read
2. Help your child learn to read
3. Develop your child's listening skills
4. Develop your child's vocabulary
5. Develop your child's reading comprehension
6. Help your child become a writer

Your child will bring home a book each day. You may use the following procedure:

1. Read the book to your child. If there is an interest, read the book a second time and encourage your child to read along. If your child is able to read alone, have him or her read the book to you. If your child is unable to read a word back to you, ask what word makes sense in that context. You will be helping your child read for meaning.

2. Talk about the book. A good way to start is to discuss whether you enjoyed the story. It would be nice if you made this a conversation rather than a question-and-answer session.

3. Share with your child something positive you noticed about her or his ability to read. Maybe she or he used pictures or the context of the text to read an unfamiliar word.

4. Return the book the next school day or as soon as possible.

Girls and homework chart.

Our classroom library collection is small, so lost books must be paid for so that replacements can be made and the Read to Me program can continue. I look forward to working with you. Together we can nurture in your child a positive attitude toward reading.

Sincerely,

Weekend Bags

I let my parents know that Weekend Bags contain materials for parent/child interactive homework. I created these bags as an enjoyable way to cover concepts that I wanted to have reinforced at home. I send these bags home over the weekend. At this point, I have enough Weekend Bags for all the students to have one. However, when I first began making them, I didn't have enough for each child to take one home every weekend, so I used a checklist and sent bags home on a rotational basis. Here are several examples of Weekend Bags.

Art Weekend Bag

This is a suitcase containing colored construction paper, scissors that cut in different ways, markers, glue, and a craft box filled with craft sticks, pompoms, beads, buttons, and sparkles. It includes the following letter to parents:

Dear Parents,

This is our art weekend bag. Please work with your child on this project. Your child will have a lot of wonderful and creative ideas. Enjoy the time with your child. Remember . . . it doesn't need to be a perfect finished product because it's the process rather than the product that is most important.

Have fun!

Three Little Pigs Weekend Bag

This is a simple canvas bag with Velcro sewn on the top to keep everything contained. This Weekend Bag contains several versions of The Three Little

Pigs story and puppets of the story characters. The following letter is included in the bag:

Dear Parents,

Remember the story of The Three Little Pigs? These days we have a variety of versions to read and compare. Hearing the story told from the wolf's point of view may make you look at him in a new light. I have included several versions of this old familiar tale. Read those that interest you and your child, and compare the different versions.

Sincerely,

Measurement Weekend Bag

This Weekend Bag connects math and literature. It contains unifix cubes, a ruler, several literature books, and a sheet suggesting objects at home to measure. The following letter is sent home in this bag:

Dear Parents,

The concept of measurement is introduced in kindergarten, and the children participate in various measurement activities throughout the year. Linear measurement is one form of measurement. Nonstandard units, such as paper clips and unifix cubes, are examples of items your child can use for measuring.

Please have your child use the enclosed unifix cubes to measure items in your home and assist him or her as needed to complete the activity sheet.

You can also read the following books: *Inch by Inch* by Leo Lionni and *Let's Measure It* by Luella Connelly. Please use the enclosed ruler to measure as you read *Let's Measure It.*

Thank you for taking the time to complete this measurement activity with your child. Enjoy!

The possibilities are endless in creating these Weekend Bags. The bags that I have created contain all the material needed for an activity related to a selected concept we are covering in school. The contents of the bags can be obtained in various ways. Many times parents have things at home that they no longer need that would be a perfect addition to a bag. If a wish list were sent home, parents would keep their eyes open for particular items. Also, most schools have a parent organization that would be willing to pur-

Kids with their Weekend Bags.

chase books for your bags. In addition, with permission from a school's administrator, requesting donations from businesses is a possibility. Weekend Bags do not have to be costly. But it takes time to create them. I began making them during the summers or when I had a break. I began with the Corduroy Weekend Bag because it was simple to make and promoted reading and writing using one of my favorite bears. I used one of my son's teddy bears and sewed some overalls with green corduroy I had found in a remnant pile at a store. The new Corduroy bear, the book about him, a journal to write what Corduroy did over the weekend, and instructions to parents were put into a canvas bag ready for the students to borrow over the weekend.

The activities in the bags are designed to promote parent interaction as well as to reinforce concepts. The contents and concepts of the bags will vary according to the needs of students in different schools. These are some of the bags I have made, and the materials in them, including directions for parents:

* Corduroy. *Corduroy* (Freeman 1968), writing journal, bear

* Three Little Pigs. *The Three Little Pigs* (Marshall 1989), *The Three Little Javelinas* (Lowell 1992), *The True Story of the Three Little Pigs! By A. Wolf* (Scieszka 1989), *The Three Little Wolves and the Big Bad Pig* (Trivizas 1993), *The Fourth Little Pig* (Celsi 1992), five different versions of the story

* Make Way for Ducklings. *Make Way for Ducklings* (McCloskey 1941), *Five Little Ducks* (Raffi 1989c), *Have You Seen My Duckling?* (Tafuri 1984), wooden duck that waddles

* Big Al. *Big Al* (Clements 1988), fiction and nonfiction ocean books

* Lunch. *Lunch* (Fleming 1993), puppet

* Ten Sly Piranhas. *Ten Sly Piranhas* (Wise 1992), tape, felt piranha, subtraction and counting backwards directions

* Three Little Bears. *Goldilocks and the Three Bears* (Brett 1987), teddy bears for counting, dolls, addition directions

* Wild Things. *Where the Wild Things Are* (Sendak 1963), rhythm instruments

* Harold and the Purple Crayon. *Harold and the Purple Crayon* (Johnson 1955), small blank books, purple crayons and pens

* "Five Little Monkeys." Poem from *Favorite Poems, Old and New* (Ferris 1957), puppets

* "The Little Turtle." Poem from *Favorite Poems, Old and New* (Ferris 1957), puppet

* Insects. *Don't Laugh, Joe!* (Kasza 1997), *What's Inside? Insects* (Royston 1992), other fiction and nonfiction insect books, play dough (see recipe in Appendix A), pan, plastic bugs to make a bug pie

* Magnets. *Magnets Concept Science* (Walker 1993), other magnet books, magnets

* Shadows. *Bear Shadow* (Asch 1985), *What Makes a Shadow?* (Bulla 1985), other fiction and nonfiction shadow books, flashlight

* Patterning. *Mr. Noisy's Book of Patterns* (Williams 1995b), other pattern books, play dough, cookie cutters to cut dough

* Plants. *Bean and Plant* (Back and Watts 1984), *From Seed to Plant* (Gibbons 1991), shovel, seeds, disposable gloves

* Counting. *Anno's Counting Book* (Anno 1975b), unifix cubes, watercolors

* Measurement. *Inch by Inch* (Lionni 1960), *Let's Measure It* (Connelly 1995), other measurement books, unifix cubes, ruler, measurement directions

* Retell a Story. Objects to use for retelling a story told in class (for example, I tell the story of Uwangalema, and African folktale, and the students retell the story at home using orange fabric for the sun, a green scarf for a tree, a plastic turtle, bear, tiger, and bird)

* Create a Story. Objects to create and write a story (for example, I include a blue washcloth, a piece of fabric netting, a pompom, a stuffed monkey, elephant, and camel)

* Art. Paper, craft items, scissors, glue

* P. E. *Jump Rope Rhymes* (Rades 1995), other books of jump rope jingles, jump ropes, sidewalk chalk, beanbag, balls

* Music. *Mother Goose's Basket Full of Rhymes* (Simon 2000), *The Book of Kid's Songs: A Holler-Along Handbook* (Cassidy and Cassidy 1986), other books of songs, tape, rhythm instruments

* If You Give a Moose a Muffin. *If You Give a Moose a Muffin* (Numeroff 1991), moose puppet, box containing objects mentioned in the story for sequencing, banana muffin recipe (see Appendix A)

End of the Year

IT IS MAY 15 AND the end of the school year is near. Reading and writing have become part of the students' everyday lives. They read and write for different purposes—entertainment, giving and gaining information, sharing and obtaining ideas, and reflecting. I am pleased with their progress.

Through their daily writing, the students now know what it takes to be a good writer: they understand the writing process. My students

* Have developed confidence and the ability to take risks
* Make choices while writing:

    How can I make it interesting?

    What should I include in this story?

    What would be an interesting word to write here?

    What would my reader want to know?

* Use a writing "voice" that has developed through reading, writing, conversation, and reflection
* Realize that writing is a process
* Apply various learned skills in their writing:

    I write my thoughts first.

    I know what to do if I need help spelling a word.

    I am choosing good words.

I start my sentences with an uppercase letter.

I have spaces between my words.

I am using periods.

This makes sense to my reader.

I reread my stories to see if I can improve them.

* Believe they are good writers.

Reading has also been very successful. Most of the students leaving my classroom are reading books with a simple text on their own. My students

* Read books of interest
* Use a variety of reading strategies appropriately when they come upon unfamiliar words:

    I look at the picture.

    I predict.

    I sound out the word.

    I look at word parts.

    I skip the word and use context clues.

    I use prior knowledge and information.

    I self-correct.

* Read and compare authors' styles
* Read all types of genres—literature books, poems, fiction, nonfiction
* Believe they are good readers

The students seek information on different topics in science and social studies through inquiry. Their research focuses on concepts within the kindergarten curriculum. In addition, the students' research topics are based upon their interests. By beginning with the prior knowledge and experience of the students, I don't reteach what they already know. In my classroom, we go far beyond the "old" ways of teaching content area material. Reading, writing, listening, and speaking are ways of learning information in the various content areas. The interests and curiosity of the children are freed by the inquiry method to power self-directed learning. The students are not dependent solely on what the teacher plans, prepares, and assigns.

In a few weeks it will be summer. The students will move on to new experiences. They leave their kindergarten year with new experiences, skills, and knowledge. Most important, they take with them a love of learning. I know my students have had great beginnings and will continue to learn and grow. I know that my theories and practice of teaching will be shaped and reshaped with every new class that I teach. My students are always teaching me, and I am eager to learn from them. I think I've had great beginnings, too.

Recipes

Applesauce

Chop 4 apples into small pieces and put into a covered pot.

Simmer in $\frac{1}{2}$ inch of water.

Add 3 tablespoons honey.

Simmer and stir until soft.

Sprinkle with cinnamon.

Banana Muffins

$\frac{1}{2}$ cup butter (room temperature)
2 eggs
$\frac{1}{4}$ cup chopped walnuts
2 cups flour

1 cup sugar
1 teaspoon baking soda
3 bananas, mashed

Cream butter and sugar.

Add eggs, nuts, and bananas.

Sift flour and baking soda, then add to mixture.

Bake in muffin pan at 350°F for 50–60 minutes.

Bubbles

1 cup warm water	1 cup warm water	½ cup warm water
2 tablespoons glycerin	¼ cup dishwashing liquid	½ cup dishwashing liquid
4 tablespoons dishwashing liquid	1 teaspoon salt	1 tablespoon cooking oil

Prepare a solution from one of the three ingredient lists.

Let stand for two days for best results.

Butter

Pour 1 tablespoon of whipping cream into a small jar.

Take turns shaking until butter forms.

Spread on crackers.

Colored Pasta

Buy bags of dry pasta in a variety of interesting shapes.

Mix the pasta and separate into large plastic bags with zipper closure.

Put several drops of red food coloring into one of the bags. Add ¼ cup rubbing alcohol.

Shake the bag well.

Spread onto cookie sheets to dry.

Repeat using other colors.

Play Dough

3 cups flour
1 ½ cups salt
3 tablespoons oil
2 tablespoons cream of tartar
3 cups water
food coloring

Mix the ingredients, making sure there are no lumps.

Cook over very low heat, stirring constantly until no longer sticky.

Put into covered containers or plastic bags with zipper closure to store.

Pretzels

1 tablespoon yeast
½ cup warm water
1 teaspoon honey
1 teaspoon salt
1⅓ cups flour
1 egg, beaten

Dissolve yeast in water.

Add honey and salt. Stir.

Add flour. Mix well.

Knead.

Roll out small pieces of dough and form into letters.

Brush with egg and sprinkle salt if desired.

Bake at 425°F for 10 minutes.

Pumpkin Seeds

After carving pumpkin, remove and wash seeds.

Spread on buttered cookie sheet.

Toast at 350°F for 10 minutes or until golden brown.

Sprinkle with salt.

Outline for Read-Aloud Workshop with Parents

Materials

A variety of children's literature for reading aloud.

Workshop Content

We begin by welcoming and thanking the families for attending the workshop. As each teacher is introduced, she or he shares a favorite children's literature book, explaining why it's their favorite and including concepts that could be emphasized. The teachers speak on the following topics.

Importance of Involvement at Home Parent involvement is of utmost importance. Children can develop a positive attitude toward reading and books when reading at home is valued and emphasized. Parents can serve as role models by regularly reading printed material such as books, newspapers, and magazines.

We are asking for parents and teachers to become partners in reading aloud to the children. Our mutual goal is to foster a love of reading. This read-aloud workshop provides guidance and strategies for reading aloud effectively and consistently.

As an African proverb says, It takes an entire village to teach a child.

Why Read Aloud? Sharing stories is fun. Just fifteen minutes of reading aloud daily can promote a lifelong love of reading. Reading, writing, and listening skills can be developed and strengthened by listening to the stories being read aloud. The vocabulary and comprehension of written language vary greatly from those of spoken language. The students' abilities can be enriched through hearing children's literature read aloud.

When to Read Aloud The best time to begin reading aloud is before a child's birth, and it should be continued long after a child has learned to read. Read-alouds should be consistently shared by designating a special and specific time, such as bedtime. When a regular time is set and a routine established, children often will remind parents or grandparents that it is time to read.

Where to Read Aloud Any place is right for reading aloud. However, a special place can be established within a routine. In addition, many public libraries offer story times.

What Kinds of Literature Are Best to Read Aloud? Many new books are published and available every year. Introduce children to a variety of genres, such as the following:

* Nursery rhymes. We all grew up with Mother Goose books. Their rhythmic and catchy language is a natural attraction.
* Alphabet and counting books. There are many different types of alphabet and counting books. *Anno's Counting Book* (Anno 1975b), *A Is for Aloha* (Feeney 1980), and *Chicka Chicka Boom Boom* (Martin and Archambault 1989) are just a few. These books will teach more than just studying numbers and alphabet letters alone.
* Picture books. In a picture book illustrations are an important part of the book. Every year several books are selected to receive the Caldecott Award. These are books chosen for their beautiful illustrations as well as for their rich text. *Swimmy* (Lionni 1963) is an example of a Caldecott Award book.
* Favorite authors. Reading books by favorite authors will accustom children to different writing styles and illustration techniques. Favorite kindergarten authors include Tomie de Paola, Eric Carle, and Mem Fox.
* Chapter books. Children always enjoy listening to chapter books,

which are longer than picture books, such as *Charlotte's Web* (White 1952). They look forward, day by day, to the next chapter.

* Poetry. Poems are usually short. It is very important to read poetry to the children. Children enjoy listening to old favorites, such as "The Little Turtle" by Vachel Lindsay (Ferris 1957), or new ones, such as those in *A Pizza the Size of the Sun* (Prelutsky 1996).

Many read-aloud resource books are available for parents, including *The New Read-Aloud Handbook* (Trelease 1989), *Choosing Books for Children: A Commonsense Guide* (Hearne 1981), and *Read to Me: Raising Kids Who Love to Read* (Cullinan 1992).

How to Read Aloud   The following are the basic steps for parents to know in reading aloud to their children:

* Before reading. When previewing the book, take a look at the cover illustration and title to make predictions about the story. Discuss the title, author, and illustrator. Most books give interesting background information about the author and illustrator on the flap of the dust jacket.
* Reading the book. While reading aloud, point to pictures and words as you read. Children enjoy joining in when there are predictable and repetitive lines, especially if the book is being read with expression.
* After reading. Once the book has been read aloud, children can be encouraged to ask questions and discuss the book. Questions such as "What was your favorite part?" or "Does this book remind you of something that happened to you?" can stimulate a meaningful discussion.

Model Reading   Reading aloud to parents at the workshop will model reading with feeling and expression. If it is a large group of parents, using a Big Book would make it be easier for all to see.

AT THE END OF THE workshop we make sure to express our appreciation to all the attendees for taking time out of their busy schedules to learn more about reading aloud to their children.

Student Information Form and Reading and Writing at Home Booklet for Parents

Student Information Form

Child's Name _____

Birthdate _____

Parents' Names _____

Address _____

Occupation of Parents

    Mother _____ phone _____

    Father _____ phone _____

Medical Insurance _____

List everyone who lives in your home:

Children's Names   Age/Relationship

_____

_____

_____

Adults' Names   Relationship

_____

_____

Please write any information that will be helpful to the teacher.

Does child have any preschool experience? _____ How long? _____

Please check things that you may be able to help with:

_____ volunteer in class   _____ field trip

_____ other (please specifiy) _____

What are your child's afterschool arrangements?

Reading and Writing at Home

Caldecott Award Books

* *Blueberries for Sal* by Robert McCloskey
* *The Funny Little Woman* by Arlene Mosel
* *The Polar Express* by Chris Van Allsburg
* *Snow* by Uri Shulevitz
* *Swimmy* by Leo Lionni

Favorite Authors

* Eric Carle
* Tomie de Paola
* Mem Fox
* Don Freeman
* Ezra Jack Keats
* Leo Lionni
* Bill Martin, Jr.
* Robert McCloskey
* Don and Audrey Wood

Dear Parents,

Remember when your child was learning to speak? He or she made many mistakes or used words that were similar but incorrect, and it didn't matter. You encouraged your child to continue to learn to speak by asking him or her questions and including him or her in conversations. As you know, children learn to speak by speaking.

Children learn to read and write the same way. They learn to read by reading. They learn to write by writing.

As you read through this booklet, I hope you will find it useful to guide you in reading and writing at home with your child.

Sincerely,

Writing

Stages of Writing

We wt a be (handwritten)

Remember when your child was learning to speak? His or her speech did not sound like the kind of speech you used. And this doesn't look like writing, at least not the kind of writing you do. However, this is writing and a wonderful beginning to a story. The child who wrote it knew exactly what it said. This child knew that written language had meaning and that what he wrote was meaningful. It reads

"We went to the beach."

Each word in the sentence is represented by one or more letters:

We wt t d be
We went to the beach.

Now let's take a look at what this child knows about writing. She or he knows that

* written language journeys across the page in a line
* written language progresses from left to right
* written language uses upper- and lowercase letters
* written language uses letters that stand for sounds in words

This is one stage of writing. There are many other stages that may come before and after this particular stage. Let's look at some of the different developmental writing stages your child may go through.

I mmm

This child is at one of the beginning stages of writing. This child is aware that language may be written. This translates into

"I like Keri's kimono."

NoiMALR

At this stage the child is using random letters to represent sound. The matching of letters with the message is not apparent. The content of the story message is not apparent. The content of the story must be committed to memory because the clues are not sufficient and the message may be lost if not listened to immediately. This story reads

"The dinosaurs make eggs."

ILMTB

This child is aware that the sounds of the letters match the symbols of the alphabet. As the child says each word, she or he writes down the first letter of each word. This reads

"I like my teddy bear."

I wous to the Krosaer

This stage is similar to the one above. The child hears the first letter of each word but is also aware that there are other letters in the word. This sentence says

"I went to the carnival."

win i giro up i ma gyi to Be q Ridror
And iMa gin To Sel Books
Pe Po We l liç My Books I am
Gw in To Mak Gorhdups Books.

This is the phonetic stage. Phonetic spellers spell words as they sound. The child perceives and delineates the letters and sounds in a word although the delineation may be unconventional. Examples would be "win" for *when*, "ridror" for *writer*. This story reads

"When I grow up I am going to be a writer and I am going to sell books. People will like my books. I am going to make grownup books."

I wish summer
School was lagr
and 3 weeks so
I will have fun.
I wish it was forevr
And I wish I
hade the sam
tehr.

This is the transitional stage where the child thinks about how words appear visually. Examples include "lager" for *longer*, "techer" for *teacher*. This story reads

"I wish summer school was longer than 3 weeks so I will have fun. I wish it was forever and I wish I had the same teacher."

The last stage would, of course, be conventional (correct) spelling.

Parts and Purposes of Writing

Children must learn the many parts and purposes of writing. They need to learn that

* written language communicates ideas from the author to the reader

* written language is made up of individual words separated by spaces

* words are made up of different letters representing different sounds

* once you know a word (such as *and*), you always spell it the same way

* if you do not know how to spell a word, you can

* use your knowledge of letters and sounds and write the letters you hear

* look around the room for the word in a label or sign

* ask someone

* look it up in the dictionary

12

Promoting Writing at Home

Children should be encouraged to write at home. Here is a list of things that children can write.

* lists—shopping, things to do, gifts

* thank-you notes

* notes to each other

* notes to grandparents or friends

* signs

* postcards

* stories about pictures they have drawn

* descriptions to go along with photos

* telephone messages

* journal of trips

* journal of summer activities

* dinner orders from family on "guest check" pad

13

Writing in Your Home

How can you help your child learn to write? Here are some ideas that you might like to try:

1. Model writing:

   * Have your child see you writing regularly.

   * Have your child see you write for different purposes (business, pleasure).

   * Make writing a positive experience.

2. Provide different opportunities for writing:

   * Set up a writing area with a supply of writing materials (writing instruments, paper, envelopes).

   * Write and illustrate weekend or summer activities in blank books.

   * Ask your child to read to you what she or he has written.

   * Sometimes ask your child to proofread what she or he has written.

   * Provide a diary or journal to write feelings and ideas (do not read this one).

   * Keep an ongoing grocery list that can be added to on the counter or refrigerator.

   * Have your child write stories on the computer and illustrate.

3. Encourage letter writing:

   * Select a comfortable and quite area.

   * Provide a variety of writing paper and envelopes.

   * Encourage writing thank-you notes or letters to grandparents or friends.

Reading

Stages of Reading

When children talk through a story and change or omit the original text, they are behaving like readers. They are going through a natural beginning reading process. Children who have memorized a text will be able to identify certain words in a story. Beginning readers also

* picture-read wordless books
* tell stories to match what they see and make predictions and inferences
* read environmental print, including
  * food labels (e.g., cereal boxes)
  * street signs (e.g., STOP)
  * signs in the community (e.g., McDonald's)

* re-read predictable books, relying first on memorization and then recognizing particular words
* build a "bank" of words they recognize on sight, e.g., *the, see, can*

Beginning readers also develop a variety of reading strategies, and you can help them do this.

Reading Strategies

We have all told our children to "sound it out" when they came upon a word they did not recognize. This is the way we were taught to read. Phonics is an important part of reading and needs to be taught. However, the primary goal of reading is to read for meaning. In order for children to become independent and fluent readers, they must know how to self-correct and scrutinize to understand the meaning of what they are reading. When your child comes upon and unknown word, do not immediately tell him or her to sound it out. Wait and see what strategies she or he uses. There are many reading strategies that a child must know in addition to "sounding it out." Through your responses, you can help your child learn some of these strategies:

* What word would make sense in the sentence?
* Use the picture to help figure out the unknown word.

* Skip over the word and read to the end of the sentence or paragraph. Then go back and see if you can figure out the unknown word.
* Put in a word that makes sense.
* See if the word was on a previous page.
* Look at the first letter of the word. For example, if it begins with a *t*, the word is likely to be *tall* rather than *big*.
* Look for word chunks. For example, in *participation*, find the chunks *par* and *tion*.
* Ask someone what the word is.

Reading in Your Home

How can you help your child learn to read? Here are some ideas that you might like to try:

1. Read to your child daily:

   * Select a comfortable and quite area.
   * Select a book that your child is interested in hearing.
   * Talk to your child about the book as you read.
   * Encourage your child to help you read part of the story.

2. Modeling reading:

   * Have your child see you reading regularly (books, newspapers, magazines).
   * Have your child see you read for different purposes.
   * Give books to your child as gifts.

   * Give books to others as gifts.
   * Visit the library regularly.

3. Provide different opportunities for reading:

   * Leave notes for your child to read on mirrors, in lunch boxes, on doors.
   * Play board games with your child.
   * Read signs as you are going places (McDonald's, Speed Limit).
   * Have your child read recipes as you bake or cook.
   * Read directions on kits together.
   * Listen to taped stories.
   * Make your own recordings of a story and listen while looking at the book.

Suggested Reading

Wordless Books

* *A Boy, a Dog, and a Frog* by Mercer Mayer
* *Do You Want to Be My Friend?* by Eric Carle
* *Deep in the Forest* by Brinton Turkle
* *Pancakes for Breakfast* by Tomie de Paola
* *Rosie's Walk* by Pat Hutchins

Nursery Rhymes

* *Humpty Dumpty and Other Rhymes* by Iona Archibald Opie
* *Mother Goose* by Michael Hague
* *The Mother Goose Songbook* by Carol Barratt
* *My Very First Mother Goose* by Rosemary Wells
* *The Real Mother Goose*, illustrated by Blanche F. Wright

Predictable Books

* *Brown Bear, Brown Bear, What Do You See?* by Bill Martin, Jr.
* *The Little Overcoat* by Yetta Trachtman Goodman
* *Love You Forever* by Robert Munsch
* *The Napping House* by Audrey Wood
* *The Very Hungry Caterpillar* by Eric Carle

Poetry

* *Animal Crackers* by Jane Dyer
* *Poems to Read to the Very Young* by Josette Frank
* *Read-Aloud Rhymes for the Very Young* by Jack Prelutsky
* *A Small Child's Book of Cozy Poems* by Cyndy Szekeres
* *Where the Sidewalk Ends* by Shel Silverstein

Children's Literature

Aardema, Verna. 1981. *Bringing the Rain to Kapiti Plain.* New York: Dial.

Ackerman, Karen. 1988. *The Song and Dance Man.* New York: Scholastic.

Anno, Mitsumasa. 1975a. *Anno's Alphabet: An Adventure in Imagination.* New York: Crowell.

———. 1975b. *Anno's Counting Book.* New York: Crowell.

Asch, Frank. 1985. *Bear Shadow.* New York: Simon & Schuster.

Aylesworth, Jim. 1998. *The Gingerbread Man.* New York: Scholastic.

Back, Christine, and Barrie Watts. 1984. *Bean and Plant.* Englewood Cliffs, NJ: Silver Burdett.

Baer, Edith. 1995. *This Is the Way We Eat Our Lunch.* New York: Scholastic.

Barabas, Kathy. 1997. *Let's Find Out About Money.* New York: Scholastic.

Barratt, Carol. 1986. *The Mother Goose Songbook.* New York: Derrydale.

Barrett, Judi. 1978. *Cloudy with a Chance of Meatballs.* New York: Atheneum.

Base, Graeme. 1986. *Animalia.* New York: Harry N. Abrams.

Blume, Judy. 1971. *Freckle Juice.* New York: Macmillan.

Bourgeois, Paulette. 1995. *Franklin Goes to School.* New York: Scholastic.

Brett, Jan. 1987. *Goldilocks and the Three Bears.* New York: Putnam.

Brown, Margaret W. 1947. *Goodnight Moon.* New York: Harper.

Bulla, Clyde Robert. 1985. *What Makes a Shadow?* New York: Simon & Schuster.

Bunting, Eve. 1994. *Flower Garden.* San Diego: Harcourt Brace Jovanovich.

———. 1999. *Butterfly House.* New York: Scholastic.

Bursik, Rose. 1992. *Amelia's Fantastic Flight.* New York: Henry Holt.

Cannon, Janell. 1993. *Stellaluna.* San Diego: Harcourt Brace Jovanovich.

Carle, Eric. 1971. *Do You Want to Be My Friend?* New York: Crowell.

———. 1972. *Rooster's Off to See the World.* Natick, MA: Picture Book Studio.

———. 1973. *Have You Seen My Cat?* New York: F. Watts.

———. 1977. *The Grouchy Ladybug.* New York: Crowell.

———. 1983. *The Very Hungry Caterpillar.* New York: Philomel.

Carlson, Nancy. 1999. *Look Out Kindergarten, Here I Come!* New York: Viking Penguin.

Cassidy, Nancy, and John Cassidy. 1986. *The Book of Kid's Songs: A Holler-Along Handbook.* Palo Alto, CA: Klutz.

Celsi, Teresa. 1992. *The Fourth Little Pig.* Austin, TX: Raintree Steck-Vaughn.

Clements, Andrew. 1988. *Big Al.* Natick, MA: Picture Book Studio.

Cohen, Miriam. 1967. *Will I Have a Friend?* New York: Macmillan.

———. 1977. *When Will I Read?* New York: Greenwillow.

Connelly, Luella. 1995. *Let's Measure It.* Cypress, CA: Creative Teaching Press.

Cousteau Society. 1991a. *Dolphins.* New York: Simon & Schuster.

———. 1991b. *Turtles.* New York: Simon & Schuster.

———. 1992. *Whales.* New York: Simon & Schuster.

Cowley, Joy. 1980. *Mrs. Wishy-Washy.* Bothell, WA: The Wright Group.

———. 1983. *The Farm Concert.* Bothell, WA: The Wright Group.

———. 1986. *I Can Jump.* Bothell, WA: The Wright Group.

———. 1989. *Mr. Grump.* Bothell, WA: The Wright Group.

Delacre, Lulu. 1989. *Time for School, Nathan!* New York: Scholastic.

de Paola, Tomie. 1973. *Nana Upstairs and Nana Downstairs.* New York: Putnam.

———. 1978. *Pancakes for Breakfast.* San Diego: Harcourt Brace Jovanovich.

———. 1981. *Now One Foot, Now the Other.* New York: Putnam.

———. 1989. *The Art Lesson.* New York: Putnam.

———. 1993. *Tom.* New York: Putnam.

De Regniers, Beatrice Schenk. 1964. *May I Bring a Friend?* New York: Atheneum.

Ditzel, Resi. 1992a. *My Pocket.* Honolulu: Bess Press.

———. 1992b. *My Slippers.* Honolulu: Bess Press.

———. 1992c. *Chinese New Year.* Honolulu: Bess Press.

Dyer, Jane. 1996. *Animal Crackers.* Boston: Little, Brown.

Feeney, Stephanie. 1980. *A Is for Aloha.* Honolulu: University of Hawaii Press.

Ferris, Helen. 1957. *Favorite Poems, Old and New.* New York: Doubleday.

Fleming, Denise. 1993. *Lunch.* New York: Henry Holt.

———. 1996. *Where Once There Was a Wood.* New York: Henry Holt.

Fox, Mem. 1985. *Wilfrid Gordon McDonald Partridge.* New York: Kane/Miller.

———. 1988. *Koala Lou.* San Diego: Harcourt Brace Jovanovich.

———. 1994. *Tough Boris.* San Diego: Harcourt Brace Jovanovich.

Frank, Josette. 1982. *Poems to Read to the Very Young.* New York: Random House.

Freeman, Don. 1968. *Corduroy.* New York: Viking Press.

Friedman, Ina. 1984. *How My Parents Learned to Eat.* Boston: Houghton Mifflin.

Gantos, Jack. 1976. *Rotten Ralph.* Boston: Houghton Mifflin.

———. 1994. *Not So Rotten Ralph.* Boston: Houghton Mifflin.

Gibbons, Gail. 1984. *The Seasons of Arnold's Apple Tree.* San Diego: Harcourt Brace Jovanovich.

———. 1991. *From Seed to Plant.* New York: Holiday House.

———. 1992. *Stargazers.* New York: Scholastic.

Goodman, Yetta Trachtman. 1998. *The Little Overcoat.* Greenvale, NY: Mondo.

Gray, Nigel. 1988. *A Country Far Away.* New York: Orchard Books.

Gretz, Susanna. 1991. *Frog in the Middle.* New York: Macmillan/McGraw-Hill.

Hague, Michael. 1984. *Mother Goose.* New York: Henry Holt.

Heard, Georgia. 1992. *Creatures of Earth, Sea, and Sky.* Honesdale, PA: Wordsong.

Heller, Ruth. 1983. *The Reason for a Flower.* New York: Grosset and Dunlap.

Hoban, Tana. 1982. *A, B, See!* New York: Greenwillow.

Hutchings, Amy, and Richard Hutchings. 1994. *Picking Apples and Pumpkins.* New York: Scholastic.

Hutchins, Pat. 1968. *Rosie's Walk.* New York: Macmillan.

———. 1970. *Clocks and More Clocks.* New York: Macmillan.

Johnson, Crockett. 1955. *Harold and the Purple Crayon.* New York: Harper & Row.

Joosse, Barbara M. 1991. *Mama, Do You Love Me?* San Francisco: Chronicle.

Kasza, Keiko. 1997. *Don't Laugh, Joe!* New York: Putnam.

Keats, Ezra Jack. 1962. *The Snowy Day.* New York: Viking.

———. 1964. *Whistle for Willie.* New York: Viking.

Laird, Donivee Martin. 1988. *The Three Little Hawaiian Pigs and the Magic Shark.* Honolulu: Barnaby Books.

Leaf, Munro. 1936. *The Story of Ferdinand.* New York: Viking.

Lionni, Leo. 1960. *Inch by Inch.* New York: Scholastic.

———. 1963. *Swimmy.* New York: Knopf.

———. 1967. *Frederick.* New York: Knopf.

———. 1968. *Biggest House in the World.* New York: Knopf.

———. 1969. *Alexander and the Wind-up Mouse.* New York: Knopf.

———. 1970. *Fish Is Fish.* New York: Knopf.

Lowell, Susan. 1992. *The Three Little Javelinas.* Flagstaff, AZ: Northland.

Marshall, James. 1989. *The Three Little Pigs.* New York: Scholastic.

Martin, Bill, Jr. 1967. *Brown Bear, Brown Bear, What Do You See?* New York: Henry Holt.

Martin, Bill, Jr., and John Archambault. 1989. *Chicka Chicka Boom Boom.* New York: Simon & Schuster.

Marzollo, Jean. 1993. *Happy Birthday, Martin Luther King, Jr.* New York: Scholastic.

Mayer, Mercer. 1967. *A Boy, a Dog, and a Frog.* New York: Dial.

Maynard, Christopher. 1995. *Mighty Machines Airplanes.* New York: Dorling Kindersley.

McCloskey, Robert. 1941. *Make Way for Ducklings.* New York: Viking.

———. 1948. *Blueberries for Sal.* New York: Viking.

Mosel, Arlene. 1972. *The Funny Little Woman.* New York: Dutton.

Munsch, Robert. 1986. *Love You Forever.* Buffalo, NY: Firefly.

Myller, Rolf. 1962. *How Big Is a Foot?* New York: Atheneum.

Numeroff, Laura. 1991. *If You Give a Moose a Muffin.* New York: HarperCollins.

Opie, Iona Archibald. 1997. *Humpty Dumpty and Other Rhymes.* Cambridge, MA: Candlewick Press.

Pfister, Marcus. 1992. *The Rainbow Fish.* New York: North-South Books.

Pinczes, Elinor J. 1993. *One Hundred Hungry Ants.* Boston: Houghton Mifflin.

———. 1995. *A Remainder of One.* Boston: Houghton Mifflin.

Prelutsky, Jack. 1984. *The New Kid on the Block.* New York: Greenwillow.

———. 1986. *Read-Aloud Rhymes for the Very Young.* New York: Knopf.

———. 1996. *A Pizza the Size of the Sun.* New York: Greenwillow.

Rades, Laura. 1995. *Jump Rope Rhymes.* Racine, WI: Western.

Raffi. 1887a. *Shake My Sillies Out.* New York: Crown.

———. 1987b. *Down by the Bay.* New York: Crown.

———. 1988. *Wheels on the Bus.* New York: Crown.

———. 1989a. *Baby Beluga.* New York: Crown.

———. 1989b. *Everything Grows.* New York: Crown.

————. 1989c. *Five Little Ducks.* New York: Crown.

Reid, Margarette S. 1990. *The Button Box.* New York: Dutton.

Rosen, Michael. 1989. *We're Going on a Bear Hunt.* New York: Margaret K. McElderry Books.

Royston, Angela. 1992. *What's Inside? Insects.* New York: DK Publishers.

Scieszka, Jon. 1989. *The True Story of the Three Little Pigs! By A. Wolf.* New York: Viking.

Sendak, Maurice. 1963. *Where the Wild Things Are.* New York: Harper & Row.

Seuss, Dr., and Jack Prelutsky. 1998. *Hooray for Diffendoofer Day!* New York: Knopf.

Shulevitz, Uri. 1998. *Snow.* New York: Farrar Straus Giroux.

Sill, Cathryn. 2000. *Insects: A Guide for Children.* Atlanta, GA: Peachtree.

Silverstein, Shel. 1974. *Where the Sidewalk Ends.* New York: Harper & Row.

Simon, Carly. 2000. *Mother Goose's Basket Full of Rhymes.* New York: Simon & Schuster.

Szekeres, Cyndy. 1999. *A Small Child's Book of Cozy Poems.* New York: Scholastic.

Tafuri, Nancy. 1984. *Have You Seen My Duckling?* New York: Mulberry.

Trapani, Iza. 1999. *Row Row Row Your Boat.* Dallas: Whispering Coyote Press.

Trivizas, Eugene. 1993. *The Three Little Wolves and the Big Bad Pig.* New York: Margaret K. McElderry Books.

Turkle, Brinton. 1976. *Deep in the Forest.* New York: Dutton.

Van Allsburg, Chris. 1985. *The Polar Express.* Boston: Houghton Mifflin.

Walker, Colin. 1993. *Magnets Concepts Science.* Cleveland, OH: Modern Curriculum.

Walsh, Ellen Stoll. 1989. *Mouse Paint.* San Diego: Harcourt Brace Jovanovich.

Walton, Rick. 1995. *Once There Was a Bull...(frog).* Layton, UT: Gibbs Smith.

Weber, Bernard. 1972. *Ira Sleeps Over.* Boston: Houghton Mifflin.

Wells, Rosemary. 1981. *Timothy Goes to School.* New York: Dial.

————. 1996. *My Very First Mother Goose.* Cambridge, MA: Candlewick Press.

————. 1998. *Yoko.* New York: Hyperion Books.

White, E. B. 1952. *Charlotte's Web.* New York: Harper & Row.

Williams, Rozanne Lanczak. 1995a. *The Magic Money Box.* Cypress, CA: Creative Teaching Press.

————. 1995b. *Mr. Noisy's Book of Patterns.* Cypress, CA: Creative Teaching Press.

————. 1995c. *The Skip Count Song.* Cypress, CA: Creative Teaching Press.

————. 1995d. *The Time Song.* Cypress, CA: Creative Teaching Press.

Wise, William. 1992. *Ten Sly Piranhas.* New York: Dial.

Wood, Audrey. 1984. *The Napping House.* San Diego: Harcourt Brace Jovanovich.

Wright, Blanche F., illus. 1944. *The Real Mother Goose.* Chicago: Rand McNally.

Professional Books

Cullinan, Bernice E. 1992. *Read to Me: Raising Kids Who Love to Read.* New York: Scholastic.

Goodman, Ken. 1996. *On Reading.* Portsmouth, NH: Heinemann.

Goodman, Yetta, and Carolyn Burke. 1985. *Reading Strategies: Focus on Comprehension.* Katonah, NY: Richard C. Owen.

Harste, J., K. Short, and C. Burke. 1988. *Creating Classrooms for Authors.* Portsmouth, NH: Heinemann.

Heard, Georgia. 1989. *For the Good of the Earth and Sun.* Portsmouth, NH: Heinemann.

Hearne, Betsy. 1981. *Choosing Books for Children: A Commonsense Guide.* New York: Delacorte.

Mills, Heidi, Timothy O'Keefe, and Diane Stephens. 1992. *Looking Closely.* Urbana, IL: National Council of Teachers of English.

Paley, Vivian G. 1981. *Wally's Stories.* Cambridge, MA: Harvard University Press.

Peterson, Ralph. 1990. *Grand Conversations: Literature Groups in Action.* New York: Scholastic.

———. 1992. *Life in a Crowded Place: Making a Learning Community.* Portsmouth, NH: Heinemann.

Routman, Regie. 1994. *Invitations: Changing as Teachers and Learners, K–12.* Portsmouth, NH: Heinemann.

Short, Kathy, and Carolyn Burke. 1991. *Creating Curriculum.* Portsmouth, NH: Heinemann.

Stephens, Diane. 1990. *What Matters? A Primer for Teaching Reading.* Portsmouth, NH: Heinemann.

Trelease, Jim. 1989. *The New Read-Aloud Handbook.* New York: Penguin.